In Praise Of Trout

DAVID PROFUMO

Foreword by Ted Hughes

ILLUSTRATIONS BY ALAN JAMES ROBINSON

VIKING

VIKING
Published by the Penguin Group
27 Wrights Lane, London W8 5TZ, England
Viking Penguin Inc., 40 West 23rd Street, New York, New York 10010, USA
Penguin Books Australia Ltd, Ringwood, Victoria, Australia
Penguin Books Canada Ltd, 2801 John Street, Markham, Ontario, Canada L3R 1B4
Penguin Books (NZ) Ltd, 182–190 Wairau Road, Auckland 10, New Zealand

Penguin Books Ltd, Registered Offices: Harmondsworth, Middlesex, England

First published 1989
1 3 5 7 9 10 8 6 4 2

Filmset in Linotron Bembo by Cambridge Photosetting Services
Printed by LEGO

A CIP catalogue record for this book is available from the British Library

ISBN 0-670-82320-1

For J.D.P. and W.M.R.,
Two Fishing Fathers

ACKNOWLEDGEMENTS

Some sections of this book have appeared previously in various forms in the *Daily Telegraph*, the *Telegraph Magazine*, and *Country Times*, and are reprinted with thanks to the Editors.

Tony Lacey and Marilyn Warnick, our Editors, are also to be thanked for their encouragement during the making of this book. I am reminded of the reply of Dr William Paley when asked by the Bishop of Durham about the progress of his latest treatise: 'My Lord, I shall work steadily at it when the fly-fishing season is over.' Nowadays, with so few close seasons, such an exercise will not wash.

CONTENTS

FOREWORD
BY TED HUGHES

One of the most fascinating things about trout is the way they fascinate men. This book tells of one man's fascination.

Do they fascinate women – in the same way? Dame Juliana wrote, I fancy, as a general, albeit perfectionist, predator. Even if I'm wrong, and she was addicted to the thought of a wild trout as to the substance of a drug, she remains one of the rare exceptions. Why have so few women confessed to this weakness in writing? I know that plenty of them are as skilled as any man, and that they are luckier, and almost as a matter of course catch bigger fish. But do they ever feel that weird, ghostly kiss at the glimpse, even at the thought, of a trout, as so many men do?

Why is the trout so fascinating, so much more so than any other fish? I ask this, having survived acute infatuations with other species. Salmon, it seems, are fascinating not because of their imaginative, ocean-going enterprise, their size, their power, their purpose, their generally brilliant, heroic behaviour, but because they are basically trout. And the passionate salmon fisher often shows a strange inclination to spoil his salmon days by spending his nights with seatrout – presumably because, as the trout of the world go, they are that bit more purist.

It seems to be a fact that the trout belongs to some special privileged order of creation. They are like the beautiful girl in the school. The school always has several attractive girls (as we now know, they are all attractive), but only rarely, and only one at a time, one who is – for some reason, for no definable reason – beautiful. All the other girls know it. All the other girls will get husbands. But she, as she blossoms, is the one that the teachers – the males without fail – recognize with a primeval touch of fear. Another! What is that small difference – which makes such an immense difference?

It can't be just the freckles. Or can it? The insect delicacy of the raiment, the unpredictable, tigerish appetite that might favour you with a swirl, the suddenly, uncannily there, the suddenly not there. Is it the 'wildness'?

A trout, certainly for me, always seems 'wilder' than any other fish. The falcon among fish. The wildness of empty hills, bleak and rocky lakes, frayed, wilderness rivers knotting into dark pools, worst weather, desolation. Those places where the great peace has an eerie sister – panic. Maybe that is why trout become, if that were possible, even more thrilling, more fascinating, in the most civilized and pampered waters. And of all the trout that haunt me, the one that disturbs me most faithfully lay there, forty-five years ago, in the Rochdale Canal, about four pounds weight, under a bridge that trembles constantly with the main traffic between Manchester and Leeds.

Every fisher falls for this Morgan Le Fay in his own way. David Profumo's text is as seductive as it well could be, fiercely arrayed in the superb illustrations by Alan James Robinson, who surely knows what I mean by that 'wildness', and who is, without a doubt, every bit as spellbound as the author. This very personal, even intimate account will stir your first pangs, your first cravings to connect with trout. And it will go far towards bewitching any who still think they can take it or leave it.

PREFACE

Of the making of fishing books there appears to be no end, and I have to confess that my heart sometimes sinks at the number of new volumes that appear every year, full of the latest information about, say, oxygen theories or developments in high-protein pastes for carp. If you tried to keep up with all these publications – each claiming to be definitive and indispensable – there would be precious little time left for visiting the waterside.

This phenomenon is not just a recent one, however. History shows that, when they are not actually fishing, anglers have always liked to read about fish – it keeps the imagination keen during the close seasons when fishermen are plotting their onslaughts for the coming year, and there are some rare books which may indeed teach you something new about the craft. But on the whole I don't believe you can learn to fish from books, and this volume is by no means a manual of instruction. Instead, it is a personal tribute (by two fanatical fishermen) to one of the most elegant and exciting fish any angler could hope to pursue, the Trout. The appeal of this fish is virtually global, since it is now established in every continent but Antarctica, and it is to be hoped that the experiences and images on which we have drawn will strike a chord with others who love the beauty of trout and the pleasure of angling for them.

Contrary to the beliefs of most laymen, anglers love fish. They spend a great deal of their time thinking about them, observing them, and trying to ensure that our waterways continue to support lively stocks of them (despite the worst efforts of modern industry and agriculture that threaten the balance of the environment). This book is more concerned with the fascinating life of the trout than with methods to secure its downfall, and there is little advice herein about tackle (which anyway is soon outdated in these days of technical innovation) or instruction on casting a fly.

In their desire to be authoritative, many angling writers seem to forget the fundamental fact that fishing is meant to be *fun*; perhaps the current vogue for competitions and prizes and record certificates, and the general fuss made in the media about landing prodigious numbers of fish, are factors that have conspired to obscure this basic element. If so, that is a shame. In the pages of this essay the joy and challenge of fishing are what concern us most – in the words of Izaak Walton, 'He that likes not the book, should like at least the picture of the Trout.'

The history of trout lore reflects an ancient affection towards this attractive fish, and not just on the part of anglers. It is proverbially associated with whole-someness and reliability – 'trusty as a trout' is an old adage, maybe owing something to alliteration along the lines of 'trusty as a Trojan', though the latter suggests gullibility rather than anything else. Thomas Coghan, in 1584, described the trout 'which is so sound in nourishing, that when we would saie in English, that a man is throughly sound, we use to say that he is sound as a Troute'.

It was also quite a common practice to keep trout in wells, many of which became revered as places of mystical significance. The real reason for doing this was to ensure the purity of the water, for not only did the fish keep it clear of insects (though seldom putting on much weight down there in the dark), but the health of the trout was also an indication that the water was clean; thus their function was similar to that of a canary down a mine-shaft. The *Westmoreland Advertiser* recorded in 1834 how a trout named Ned had been placed in a well by a boy and lived there for 53 years, fed by hand by its original captor until a drought killed it off; tall stories about this fish exist in abundance, too.

Because of its exuberance and trim physical splen-dour, the trout was also involved in certain traditional fertility rites. The ancient Celts celebrated the rebirth of the sun and the passing of the dead months of winter with a dance of 'the springing trout', wherein the leaping fish-dancers imitated the rising fish to repre-sent the sun rising from the water. The trout as a motif of health and fertility is a familiar one in European culture.

One further, popular association is worth mention-ing: the fish's susceptibility to 'tickling' or 'guddling', a technique known to poachers which involves un-obtrusively stroking the fish until it is lulled suffici-ently to be flipped out on to the bank. Folk wisdom, which has always betrayed a healthy strain of sexu-ality, adapted this propensity of the trout for lascivious innuendo. Signor Claudio in Shakespeare's *Measure For Measure* is packed off to prison for 'Groping for trouts in a peculiar river', and such traditional wisdom enjoyed a very wide currency until killed off by the Age of Reason – once dubbed 'the shortest damn Age in history'. Many of our favourite nursery rhymes contain such veiled allusions to the sexual nature of fishing and poaching, for example the tale of Tom Tittle-Mouse who 'caught fishes in other men's ditches'. The association of fishing and amatory adventures has a long history.

Trout used to be kept in wells, to ensure the purity of the water

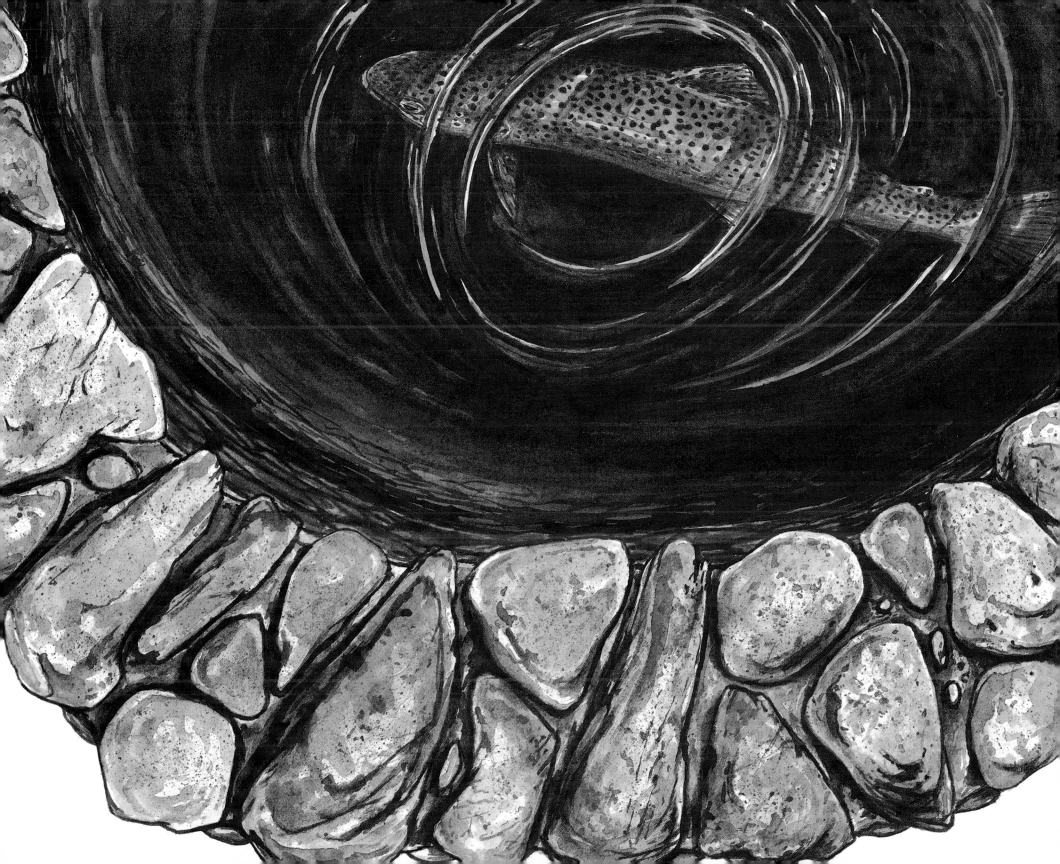

Here is Coghan again, speaking of the trout: 'This fish of nature loueth flatterie; for being in water it will suffer it selfe to be rubbed and clawed, and so to be taken. Whose example I would wish no maydes to follow, lest they repent after clappes.'

Man has found the trout an obliging and fascinating fish in many ways, and for hundreds of years. It has long been prized as a table fish and as a sporting quarry, and, because it is so adaptable to laboratory conditions, a lot more is known about its behaviour than is the case for most species. Like all fish, however, it remains a creature of a certain mystery to scientists and anglers alike. It is in some ways an archetypal freshwater fish in behaviour and appearance, and any study of its characteristics will suggest aspects in common with other species of interest to the sportsman.

But for us it is *the* fish, endlessly intriguing in its many different shapes and forms. In what follows, we have not attempted to be exhaustive in covering its thousands of habitats worldwide; instead, we have concentrated on what we know of trout in Britain and America. Those intent on studying in depth subjects only touched upon here may pursue their reading through the books listed in the Bibliography. Our prime concern, to cite Walton once again, is 'that in writing of it I have made myself a *recreation* of a *recreation*'.

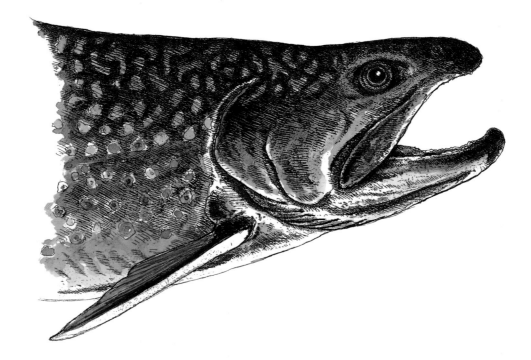

Brook trout

APOLOGIA
THE MYSTIQUE OF FISHING

*After the doctor's departure Koznyshev expressed the wish
to go to the river with his fishing rod. He was fond of
angling and was apparently proud of being fond of such a
stupid occupation.*

Leo Tolstoy: ANNA KARENINA

I am obsessed by fish, and I freely confess it. The walls of my house are hung with pictures of them and I sport their image on everything from belt-buckles to beer-mats. In the bathroom that is the noisy province of my children I have installed a musical-box with a trout that rocks to the rhythm of 'As Time Goes By' – designed, perhaps, as a reminder of life's ever-rolling stream. I have fish on my braces, shirts, swimming-trunks, pen-holders, plates and coffee-mugs. On any given day of the week, if I went under a bus, the unfortunate driver would at least be able to tell that I had been a keen angler.

Fishing for fun, rather than merely for sustenance, dates from around 2000 B.C., making it a practice twice as old as Christianity, a faith with which it was for many centuries closely identified. Ambrose Bierce defined overwork as 'a dangerous disorder affecting high public functionaries who want to go fishing', but in reality it is a fever that seems to afflict all types and estates of men – and of women, too, for the female angler is generally deadlier than the male, once her mind is committed to the sport – irrespective of vocation or background.

It also knows few geographical limits. From the trout of the Atlas Mountains to the salmon of Alaska, from the billfish of tropical seas to the tiddlers of the Thames, anglers pursue their quarry with what can only be described as fanatical devotion. And angling is no respecter of age, either, for it can be indulged in from virtual infancy until the flesh has grown weak. My own early mentor was an uncle who was still fishing into his nineties, and many are the devoted anglers who have departed this life during a fishing trip, some, according to authentic accounts, while in the very act of landing their last fish.

All of which seems quite baffling to the uninitiated,

who generally regard anglers as harmless cranks or deranged figures of fun. Yet today it is one of the world's most popular pastimes: there are 20 million anglers in Japan, three million in Britain, and a staggering 46.6 million in the United States – that's one in four of the population. And during a single week last summer, American fishermen spent $25 million on tackle – a rate of $2,500 per minute. Whatever the attraction, it is clearly more than a minority interest.

The question is this – are fishermen mad? Certainly many people have thought so, and a steady stream of satire and cartoonery supports the view. To the outsider, the angler appears to be a sedentary, sculptural figure over whom the rain pours and the wind blows as he perches on some lonely bank before returning, empty handed, at dusk, full of whisky and incomprehensible anecdotes. He is a creature of superstition who each winter surrounds himself with books over which he pores like some astrologer with his charts, and in the clement months he disappears entirely, to take some wilderness cure of an arcane nature.

Most anglers would admit they suffer from this '*amabilis insania*': the Duc de Choiseul came clean in 1761 and accepted that '*La Pêche est ma folie*', and the sport has certainly had its fair share of eccentrics. Thomas Birch, an aptly named Keeper of Books at the British Museum in Victorian times, used to disguise himself elaborately as a tree, hoping to fool the trout that his casting arm was a bough waving in the wind (he was eventually laughed out of his camouflage by friends concerned for his sanity). Jonathan Raban has recounted how the great American poet Robert Lowell used to spend most of his trout-fishing time floundering about in the water; while the late Esmond Drury (a pioneering angler who invented a revolutionary treble hook for salmon) in 1953 won a bet by casting a line from the roof of the Savoy Hotel over the trees and into the Thames (he was secured by a window-cleaner's harness, to combat his vertigo).

Among the many popular myths and misconceptions about angling we should perhaps single out the following: first, that there is some vague affiliation known as the 'brotherhood of the angle'. This is simply not true, alas. When away from the water, anglers are indeed convivial with one another; understandably, they seek out each other's company as a source of solace and respite in the nightmare clutter of our cities, to parley and dream about where they would rather be. But at the waterside the angler is generally an individualist; he has gone there to escape from the enervating preoccupations of everyday life, to sweep away the lumber and cobwebs that are so successfully accumulated by phone calls, tax-demands and queueing at length somewhere for something you do not really want. The neophyte who expects any other fisherman he encounters to fall into protracted discourse is often mortified to discover that Waltonian dialogue is a thing of the past, and that the best he can hope for is a brief appraisal of the weather.

Another myth is that the angler is attuned in some special way to the minutiae of his natural surroundings. This is another legacy of that Golden Age of angling literature, the seventeenth century, when the pace of life was less frenetic and dire. Fishermen are still rather keen to preserve this notion of a peculiar communion with nature, and, while there indubitably are some anglers who have developed skills of observation and watercraft that allow them access to the rhythms and tiny idiosyncrasies of what is happening at any given time around and upon the water, most of us are so absorbed with trying to untangle a bird's nest of nylon, or choosing the next change of fly from the box, that we probably wouldn't notice if a fish-eagle came and nested on our deerstalker headgear.

In my experience, communing with nature plays a very small part in a day's fishing, except in as much as one desperately wants to discover what the recalcitrant fish are feeding on. Of course it is a bonus to be spending time in the countryside – and the places where one goes fishing are often very beautiful indeed – but when I am fishing I concentrate on fish. Anglers are at best only flawed types of naturalist, anyway, because they want to get down in there among it all, among the weeds and the bugs and the currents, and turn things to their advantage. Nor, in the end, are they concerned to learn all the answers as to what makes a fish take a lure under particular circumstances, or how the whole complex of the subsurface world operates with its own intriguing logic. Anglers have a vested interest in preserving a certain measure of mystery about these things, and this is, thankfully, an inevitable state of affairs.

Probably the most common stigma attached to anglers is that they are prone to exaggeration, if not downright mendacious. Personally, I have found most to be remarkably honest, but there are always exceptions. As Morley Roberts once wrote: 'Among a hundred bishops there are a few who steal umbrellas and Elzevirs.' The idea that fishermen spend their time spinning yarns about the ones that got away is quite false: on the whole, other anglers simply won't put up with it, and the braggart at the bar who has a dozen tales of close encounters that would, but for mischance rather than ineptitude, have earned him an enduring place in the annals of the sport wins himself only the pity or contempt of his reluctant audience.

What then is the essence of this pastime that fills the waking hours of otherwise responsible people and transports them to a dimension wherein other mental concerns seem to be suspended for a crucial, restorative interlude? Considering the millions of words that have been written on the subject of fish and fishing, very few concerted attempts have been made to explain this enigma, and I will be bold enough only to submit two factors which I believe lie close to the heart of the sport.

First, there is the element of unpredictability, which is surely the quintessence of the whole business. Angling is largely to be distinguished from other field sports because the connivance of the quarry is required at the *moment critique*, and the central act is one of deception rather than one of marksmanship or pursuit – though, to be sure, those are also involved to varying degrees. Very often you cannot be certain as to either the number or the kinds of fish you are fishing over at any given moment, nor can you predict what size of fish you may find yourself connected to when something takes hold of your lure. There might be nothing out there, or something of which you have only ever dreamed.

Pheasant tail nymph

And this brings us to the second factor, though it is not one I can prove; if I am preaching to the converted, you will surely recognize it at once. In that mixture of simultaneous concentration and relaxation that goes with the experience of angling, there is an act of imagination at work that is quite unique. You not only think *about* the fish, but also *like* the fish, as nearly as your powers of mental displacement will permit. As we shall see in a later chapter, this peculiar circuitry accounts for the other-worldliness of much angling experience; but fishermen are often reluctant to discuss it, in case it sounds over-fanciful. It certainly sounds crazy to an outsider – but then so, to me, does the pastime of collecting Camembert cheese labels (tyrosemiophily). And don't talk to me of golf, or train-spotting.

Although the remainder of this book is devoted to the qualities of one fish in particular, I firmly believe that, for any angler worth his salt, the experiences of fishing for different species are transferable paradigms – that is, distinct variations of the same essential process. Until about a hundred years ago few distinctions and sub-divisions were made in this potentially democratic sport, and the concept of 'an all-round angler' was taken for granted. But a pernicious snobbery arose in England at the height of the Victorian era, the legacy of which still lingers in some circles – namely, the distinction drawn between 'game' and 'coarse' fish.

Coarse fish have been so designated because of their inferior table qualities, and today in Britain hardly any of them are taken for food. On the Continent, where tastes are more catholic, carp, perch and pike are often retained as a matter of course to grace a *ragoût* or *quenelle*, and these species are quite properly accorded the admiration and respect they deserve. I have nothing against specialist anglers of any type, but to hear (as one still does) intricate and skilful methods of angling, such as float-fishing for roach, being dismissed by those in whose opinion a dry-fly for trout is the only valuable form of fishing is a monstrous hangover from Imperialist days long gone. I dislike all snobbery, but that strain bred of ignorance is the least acceptable of all.

One of the glories of angling is surely the sheer variety of experience on offer, and the dedicated *fanatico* will tailor his other commitments so that he gets to cast a line, wherever he may be in the world. Whether or not there may be a field marshal's baton in every private's rucksack, there are certainly travelling rods secreted in the luggage of many international captains of industry. On one particular occasion in my life I was rather pleased at my own ingenuity in this respect. It was, in fact, on my honeymoon. Having assured my wife that we were going somewhere agreeably hot, the precise location of which would be a surprise until we reached the airport (like many fishermen, I am a romantic at heart), we flew to India. This is a very large country, and there is a lot to see in a fortnight; but I managed to invent a proverb – which I claimed to be a translation from Gaelic – that predicted any marriage would last for ever if the couple went fishing directly after the ceremony.

Although she comes, reluctantly, from a family in which the tradition of fishing is unshakeably strong, and though no one could conceivably accuse her of

'Fishing is a kind of hunting by water'

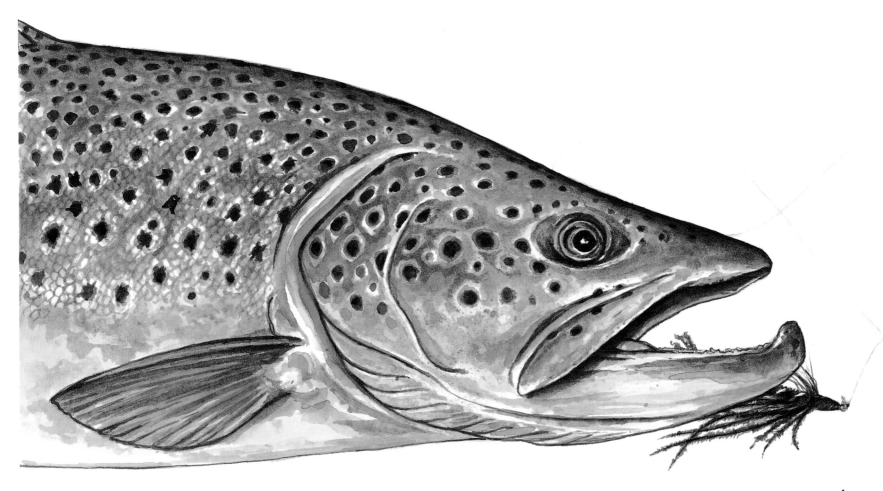

Any marriage would last forever if the couple went fishing directly afterwards

being an angler, my wife seemed to be understanding when we arrived in Kashmir on the opening day of the trout season. We fished the Lidder River, still swollen with snow-melt and unappetizingly high for the fly-fisherman; and on the very first morning I caught a brown trout of 3½ pounds on a Peacock Streamer, and it made a most welcome addition to the bland nursery cuisine that was otherwise the staple fare on our houseboat on Lake Dal.

Tolerance was stretched, however, on our return. That doyen of chalk-stream anglers, Dermot Wilson, had generously offered us a day on his hallowed beat of the Test at Kimbridge during the mayfly season; to me, this was the finest of all wedding presents, but there was some early dissension in the ranks. We went, of course, and, while I blundered around in indecision about which of the hundred fish rising at any one time I should address with my fly, Dermot soon had Helen attached to a rainbow in excess of four pounds, an achievement that he immortalized on celluloid for subsequent exhibition. It all seemed most unfair.

However, angling is not a pursuit that requires the recognition of others to justify its practice. It is only rarely a spectator sport and has never been a branch of chivalry or an exclusively aristocratic preserve, such as hunting or hawking, at which onlookers traditionally gathered in order to admire one's skills as a Renaissance Man. Anglers tend to go about their business privately – where they can, in these times of massive demand for access to the water – and in the end they don't much care whether others think them mad or not. Thomas Tod Stoddart, the indefatigable Victorian writer from the Scottish Borders who was labelled 'the Poet Laureate of Angling' by John Buchan, was approached in later life by someone with whom he had been at school and who desired to know what he was now doing. 'Doing? *Doing?*' replied the sage. 'Mon, I'm an *angler*.'

European brown trout
(Salmo trutta fario)

SMALL BEGINNINGS
THE TROUT AND THE CHILD

I remember when I was a little boy, I felt a great fish at the
end of my line which I drew up almost on the ground, but it
dropt in, and the disappointment vexeth me to this very day,
and I believe it was the type of all my future disappointments.

Jonathan Swift: CORRESPONDENCE

Anglers are said to have notoriously selective memories: successfully captured fish display remarkable posthumous growth; little details concerning the success of others are omitted from record books; blank days become conflated with rosier ones, so that with time the past appears an idyllic patchwork of outings when the trout rose porpoise-like until late in the afternoon – human luncheon having had to be postponed – and virtually each cast went straight and true.

Most fishermen are indeed idealists at heart, and we all tend to look back on earlier years as having consisted of better days, when fish were more numerous and angling pressure was slighter. There is nothing new in this, of course: Thomas Bastard was complaining about just the same thing in the sixteenth century: 'But now the sport is marde, and wott ye why? Fishes decrease, and fishes multiply.' Grumbling about a general decline in standards is an in-

eradicable badge of human behaviour.

But there is one particular occasion that the angler's memory will preserve for ever in all the bright accuracy of its true detail, and that is the day when he caught his first fish. It is a peculiarly private and intimate memory, and not one he will discuss freely unless he is in company which he knows he can trust not to sully it in some way by ridicule or indifference; for it is a precious dream, an encapsulation of all the tribulations and triumphs that have since intervened in his busy angling life.

Time and again in fishing literature one comes across luminous descriptions of such reminiscences – indeed, they are probably the single best feature that such books have in common – and although they may be fancifully coloured by an allowable measure of nostalgia, they usually breathe the true spirit of the sport. The capture of that first fish is something that, as Stoddart says, 'hangs within the Mind's dark gallery'.

And there must be millions of people for whom the first taste of angling success came courtesy of an obliging trout. Childhood fishing is often a business of tangles and tantrums and, if one is as unlucky as Dean Swift, tears of frustration as well (he might have taken solace, being a philosopher, from Cotton's Piscator, who advised on a similar occurrence: 'Nay, the *Trout* is not Lost, for pray take notice no man can lose what he never had'). In the background there is generally some elder statesman of the angle in attendance to avert drowning and to assist with knots, and this figure, too, will go down in your personal mythology in the way that all really influential teachers do. He may be a mauve-faced ghillie muttering against the midges from beneath his cap, or a benign godfather who has sacrificed a day after salmon to discharge his pastoral duties; but either will be as pleased as Punch if the novice lands a fish, because the chances are that as a result he will find himself hooked for life as an angler.

While I was writing this book, my elder son, James, caught his first ever fish at the age of four. It was not a trout – we had tried once before for trout, but conditions were against us and I called it a day before he became too disillusioned. What he caught was a small perch on a spun lure in a New Hampshire pond. Up until the time he caught it I had assumed he was only going through the motions of enthusiasm in order to keep me happy or to imitate what he thought adults did when they were trying to be especially grown up, but the minute he realized what had actually happened a glow of such pride suffused his face that I recognized with a sudden clarity my own reaction at a similar moment some thirty years before.

My trout-fishing career begins with an elderly Land-Rover clanking to a halt by a little bridge on a lonely moor in the Highlands of Scotland. After several days of rain, the water of the swollen burn that bustled down through the tweedy landscape was stained as dark as stout, with creamy foam twindling in the eddies. A sceptical boy of five, equipped with a rudimentary plastic rod of dubious foreign pedigree (it had, I recall, a bright yellow handle), a battered fly-reel loaded with thick nylon, an outsize cork bung that looked as if it would take a pike to submerge it, and a tobacco-tin filled with worms scoured in sphagnum moss, I bent dutifully to my task.

To be honest, I expected to catch nothing; to my untutored eye it didn't look much of a place, and I couldn't recall anyone else being in a hurry to fish there. I suppose I was thinking more of my tea, as the orange float bumbled down below the bridge and disappeared under water. Seconds later a diminutive trout was flying back over my head into the heather behind me, and from that moment on I was unstoppable in my efforts.

I often think of that trout, and of its twin which I took some short time later. They were unlucky to be caught, since the large salmon-hook I was using could scarcely be accommodated within their mouths, and I doubt the point even penetrated them through the bulge of lobworm with which it was baited. But there is a photograph of me in my sensible grey anorak displaying my two glittering prizes – slightly at arm's length, as the inexperienced angler will – and they look

Both child and trout are hooked for life

as beautiful to me today as they did then. Neither could have weighed more than six ounces, and they were dark as mahogany, long and streamlined and large-eyed, studded with red spots. In retrospect, it might have been but a minor triumph; at the time, I felt sure that the entire universe was holding its breath at my singular achievement.

Some anglers forget their delight experienced in such small captures; but the true fisherman retains a lifelong affection for little trout and other tiddlers, releasing them with care and admiration on later occasions when they are hooked unintentionally. There was a time, he remembers, when such a fish would have been an enviable catch, and so he returns it lovingly to the water. The world has changed for the angler since those days, but he is mindful of the importance of small beginnings for both quarry and man. The two part company; they will grow older and wiser. The fisherman hopes they will meet again.

I am always suspicious of those anglers who gauge the success of their sport merely by the criterion of avoirdupois. Many so-called experts would do well to take a refresher course in tiddler fishing to remind themselves that success is always relative to the water being fished, and a half-pound trout from a food-poor moorland stream is as much a trophy as – perhaps even more than – a double-figure jumbo stockfish caught lumbering round the margins of a small purpose-built stillwater prison.

One of the great things about doing something in the company of a child, is, of course, the way in which it refreshes your own often jaded vision of things. Children have a capacity for wonder, and a simultan-eous lack of inhibition in showing it, that is greatly invigorating to the adult who, through familiarity, has become fixed in his outlook. Take a child to the aquarium in a zoo and he will be spellbound by the strangeness of fish, moving with undiminished enthusiasm from tank to tank, pointing in both curiosity and amusement. The cynic might say that he imagines he is watching television; but the truth is that the sight of these unfamiliar creatures, presented in such tantalizing and close proximity, excites a basic and common fascination in most human beings.

And so-called 'grown-ups' are no better, especially if they happen to be anglers. Gazing at fish, however sacrosanct and untouchable, is a favourite pastime that surely goes back to a childhood preoccupation with chasing shadows; for most anglers, like children, are idealists who love to fantasize and make up stories for themselves about what may or may not be happening in the invisible world. For a child – at any rate, for a happy one – this applies to most things in his all-too-short years of innocence, but the fisherman must seek out precious moments to recapture and re-create this wonder and speculation about a world in which, for a while, adult concerns of ugliness and the diurnal pressure of clocks and schedules have no place. He re-enters the clear, underwater dream of a world that is focused and simplified and yet still pregnant with mystery of an unthreatening kind. After such a session of fishing, the mind seems extraordinarily cleansed, as writers on the subject have observed since the Middle Ages: 'For it shall cause hym to be holy and to the heele of his body; For it shall cause him to be hole.'

When I think of the transporting effect of merely

looking at fish without the least prospect of casting for them, three locations of captive trout spring to mind. The first is a culvert beside the High Street in Hampshire's fabled Stockbridge (the *locus classicus* of much chalk-stream fishing, and base of the legendary Houghton Club). A carrier of the River Test flows strong and clear under the road and, for ten yards or so, forms a pool between the tarmac and the pavement. Here reside, in absolute safety, rainbows, brown trout and grayling of prodigious size that are effectively pets of the township. By coincidence, there is now a large Orvis shop but a fly's cast from this spot; and one can hardly conceive of a greater natural inducement to dash off and purchase all sorts of unnecessary tackle than the prior sight of these inviolate but wild specimens quivering just a few yards from the emporium.

Altogether more deliberate is the ploy in evidence at the renowned stillwater fishery of Avington, near Winchester. This venue, which has established itself as a byword for huge, selectively reared rainbows (of which more later) and which holds several records for fly-caught fish, has located the stewponds containing some of its largest trout directly in front of the parking-lot. You don't have to be a child to experience the hand-shaking excitement at seeing vast double-figure trout plunge and swirl as you try to concentrate on tackling-up; and of course it is a very good advertisement for the size of fish that the farm is capable of producing. Whether or not you actually get to see anything of similar proportions in the lakes you will be paying to fish, you will have seen trout sizeable enough to disturb your sleep for many a night.

Lastly, there is a lovely stretch of the Wiltshire Avon where the main flow has been diverted through a millpond, and the water that emerges below the building is preserved as a quiet sanctum for fish that the owners do not intend to molest. In the vodka-clear water you can observe the browns and rainbows feeding and finning to their hearts' content, performing without fear of your shadow every rise-form you see pictured in books, a perfect aquarium for dawdling over while the mind wanders under water. Not far away are the wild fish to tax your reserves of patience and stamina, for they are extremely hard to catch; and it is most galling to return, empty handed, past these privileged pets after hours spent flogging the water without success. Even the most fair-minded of anglers is tempted to have just one cast, under the circumstances.

Most of what I learned about fishing as a child was gleaned from the pursuit of trout, but I also enjoyed a brief period of apprenticeship as a coarse-fisherman. This happened, appropriately enough, on the River Lea at Ware in Hertfordshire, the precise place where Izaak Walton was headed in his classic work on the subject. Here I learned the delicate art of float-fishing for roach and perch, and also how to capture freshwater crayfish with a dropline and net. Further opportunities to try different types of angling were available at Eton, a college which can boast among its advantages a very fine stretch of the River Thames, which I used to fish assiduously when scholastic timetables permitted.

Since I was absolutely hopeless at the compulsory games that were then still the benchmark of schoolboy

Roach   Perch   Carp   Pike

success, my great ambition was to win the cup for the largest trout caught from the college water in any given season. I cannot remember exactly when a boy had last qualified for this trophy, but it must have been a good forty years before I was there, in those days when the Thames trout was a celebrated and well-distributed species in weirs and locks, and there were still professional Thames fishermen who would take you out in punts to angle for them. In the way that such things happen in an enclosed community, word got around that a large brown trout had been seen rolling by the confluence of the main river and a tributary, and a party of us would set out, whenever possible, to catch it and secure immortal reputation. We fished bleak livebait on flyrods, and caught many pike, but we were eventually banned by the school authorities who, in their wisdom, reckoned we were really fishing for coarse species out of season. And so I never won any kind of cup.

But, as many gamefishers appreciate, coarse-fishing techniques can provide a very useful grounding when it comes to hunting the salmonid. Those who chase coarse species are aware of the need for stealth and the necessity of frequently fishing fine; they are also instinctively conscious of the varying depths at which a bait may be fishing – something that the gamefisher will ignore at his peril. My own fishing progress concentrated hereafter upon trout, and though there have subsequently been hundreds of exciting experiences with salmon, tuna and pike, I regard myself as a trout-fisherman.

Before I became even a teenager I was lucky enough to have regular access to two quite distinct types of

Trout anglers should never be snobs: many coarse fish are handsome and powerful

trout fishing, from both of which I learned by trial and error. Such lessons stay with you for ever. I have already mentioned the venerable uncle who was my early mentor; an expert shot and an extremely experienced fisherman, he had also that talent for exciting the interest of a child without appearing to be bored or being patronizing, which is the first thing that will deter a novice and send him back to his Dinky cars. For several summers my father and he took the leases on various sporting estates in Sutherland, until my uncle finally bought a place of his own, by Rogart in Strathfleet.

It was in the spate waters of the Fleet that one day, at thirteen, I landed my first Atlantic salmon; but I spent longer hours trying the tributary of the Lettie Burn that flowed into it. The trout here were tiny, but fishing the miniature falls and glides with a small cane rod and a sparsely hackled spider pattern on a size-14 hook demanded cunning and stealth, qualities which at first I lacked entirely. The things I remember most were the freedom of working my way up this precipitous stream for hours with no one else in sight, struggling to get the short casts to snake out correctly without splashing and so spooking the residents, chancing the sideways flick under the rowans, and scrambling back to the lodge, filled with joy when I had landed a trout worth keeping for breakfast. I will always remember the exquisite feeling of pride I experienced when seeing one of my little fish, grilled and crispy and white-eyed in the dish on the hot-plate next morning. That, and the ache of the cold water of the Lettie Burn in my throat as I slaked my thirst. My uncle died before this book was finished – but he would have relished the idea that his humblest burn was being celebrated.

Down south in Hertfordshire I was no less fortunate in my piscatorial education, for we lived on a farm at the far extent of which was an overgrown chalk-stream called the River Rib. The kindly farmer who owned this land belonged to the dying breed of dog-and-stick proprietors, and he seemed to have little or no interest in the commercial development of his assets. He was certainly no fisherman, but allowed me to ply his water for free throughout the season. As a result, I had some eight years of unrestricted and exclusive access to a magical half-mile of clean, challenging and trout-bearing water; and it was here, I think, I won my spurs as a trout-fisher, and passed from angling childhood to relative maturity.

When I say the Rib was overgrown I mean that, except in one section, our beat was so overhung with trees and bushes that it was quite impossible to cast a fly. So slow-moving and narrow was it, also, that wading upstream to switchcast (assuming even that I could have done it) was quite out of the question. When first I ventured to the river, at the age of eleven, to spy out its pools, I was horrified at the size of the brown trout I could see there. They were enormous. I had never seen trout alive, in the water, of such a size. Although one could spot only one fish in every pool, and each pool was about the size of a farmhouse table, they appeared to be vast specimens – especially to a young angler who was hitherto used only to the more stunted natives of a Highland burn.

But these trout were no beauties, except in terms of size. Whether or not they were native fish or residuals from some long-forgotten stocking elsewhere I do not know (certainly no trout had been introduced into his particular stretch, in the farmer's recollection), but it was pretty clear that they had seldom been fished for. Never since have I seen brown trout like them. They were thin and long, and had huge heads, like pike. Their backs were of a rather pale green, but the flanks were the golden colour of a light malt whisky, with a very few large splodges of chocolate brown. They had the lean and hungry look of carnivores (the expression 'old trout', so cruelly applied to ladies of a certain age, suddenly seemed to make sense as one watched them gulping and probing in the current), and I never saw one that could have been less than two pounds.

It took me some time to work out how to catch them, because it was difficult to approach any pool, despite the cover of foliage, without sending the single resident darting under the safety of one of the many tree-stumps, from which it would not emerge for ages. I winkled one or two out on a leaded nymph, and one on a dapped cranefly, but on the whole they were not responsive to the artificial fly. Every day when I was at home, from April to September, I would go down to the river and creep up and down the pools; like some shepherd with his flock, I came to know every trout that lay in our reach, and gradually I pulled them out, one by one.

As time went by and I became more ambitious, I persuaded my father to get permission to try the stream with an experimental stock of rainbows, but these either got caught at once or disappeared. Still there remained the elusive, jade-and-gold trout: I had caught them up to 3½ pounds, I had poached fish from

They had the lean and hungry look of carnivores…

the nearby stretches in the evening, I had deployed every lure from midge pupae to dead minnows – on a chalk-stream, but I admit it – and still there were some that eluded me.

For each trout I actually landed, I suppose I must have spent about two weeks fishing: such a rate of return gives an idea of my early obsession and an indication of the hours I passed simply watching and plotting. There were very few fish in the stretch, and you only had a couple of chances (if that) at each one every day. Needless to say, there was one particularly large one that I desperately wanted to catch, but he lived by a jam of fallen logs, and only once did I succeed in putting a bait over him – it was a natural minnow-tail – which he inspected and then ignored. I used to daydream about the challenge of that fish when I was supposed to be doing important things like trigonometry.

And then, one Boxing Day, when we were out shooting and I was the flank gun walking along the river I found his corpse by the rushes, just downstream of the log-jam that had been his home. There was a spearmark through his skull, so he had evidently been taken by a heron in one of his few unwary moments; but the flesh was not otherwise attacked, and the predator must have been scared off shortly after securing its prize. I looked at the trout's carcass with a mixture of envy and regret: he must certainly have weighed six pounds, and this was in the winter, when he was out of condition. I had always thought of him as my private fish, and I felt cheated.

One of the worst things about remembering waters that were pleasant and productive for you when you were a child is that they can be changed utterly in so short a time. The section of the Rib that I recall with such fondness was shortly afterwards shorn of its trees and had its banks sliced, presumably to improve its drainage potential. We moved from Hertfordshire but, when a few years later I revisited the Highland burn where first I fell under the glamorous spell of the trout, I saw that this had suffered a similar fate. The nutbrown water now came regularly down through the moor in a kind of featureless canal and passed under that bridge through a section of concrete pipe. To my mind's eye, the ghost of the aeons-old burn still snaked its way through the outcrops of peat that had vanished, and I recalled the exciting 'glug' of its tiny pools as I first approached it.

But no small boy will catch trout there again. This is called Progress.

There was a spearmark through his skull

A COAT OF MANY COLOURS
THE APPEARANCE AND VARIETY OF TROUT

I would glide down the rivulet of quiet life, a Trout.

S. T. Coleridge: NOTEBOOKS

All the world's species of trout belong to the *Salmonidae* family, a tribe of vertebrate fishes which, as their name suggests, also includes the salmon. They first appeared on the evolutionary obstacle course about 70 million years ago during the Eocene period of the Cenozoic era.

The European brown trout, *Salmo trutta fario*, is a prime example of a fish that has proved highly successful at evolutionary adaptation. We tend perhaps to take such things for granted, but not all creatures are so happily suited to their environments; the Giant Panda, for instance, suffers terribly from indigestion because it feeds upon bamboo but is equipped with the alimentary tract of a carnivore. The trout, however, is versatile in the extreme and is at one with its environment, where humans have left this possible.

Brownies are naturally distributed from the White Sea in the north to the southerly Mediterranean, including Morocco and the Atlas Mountains, and from the Aral Sea in the east as far west as the Atlantic, including Ireland. They are to be found thriving across Europe in Alpine lakes and streams, across Russia in the Black and Caspian Seas and as far as the Hindu Kush. There exist at least a dozen subspecies on the Continent, and everywhere they are distinguished by local variations in colour and profile.

The brown trout is a cold-water species, and it is probable that these widespread populations became established at the end of the last glacial period. As the ice receded once again northwards, the migratory instinct led some fish to follow it, while others ascended rivers and streams in search of cooler water, some eventually becoming landlocked. There is some evidence that the Mediterranean was once very much colder than it is now, and subspecies such as *S. trutta*

Rainbow trout (Salmo gairdneri)

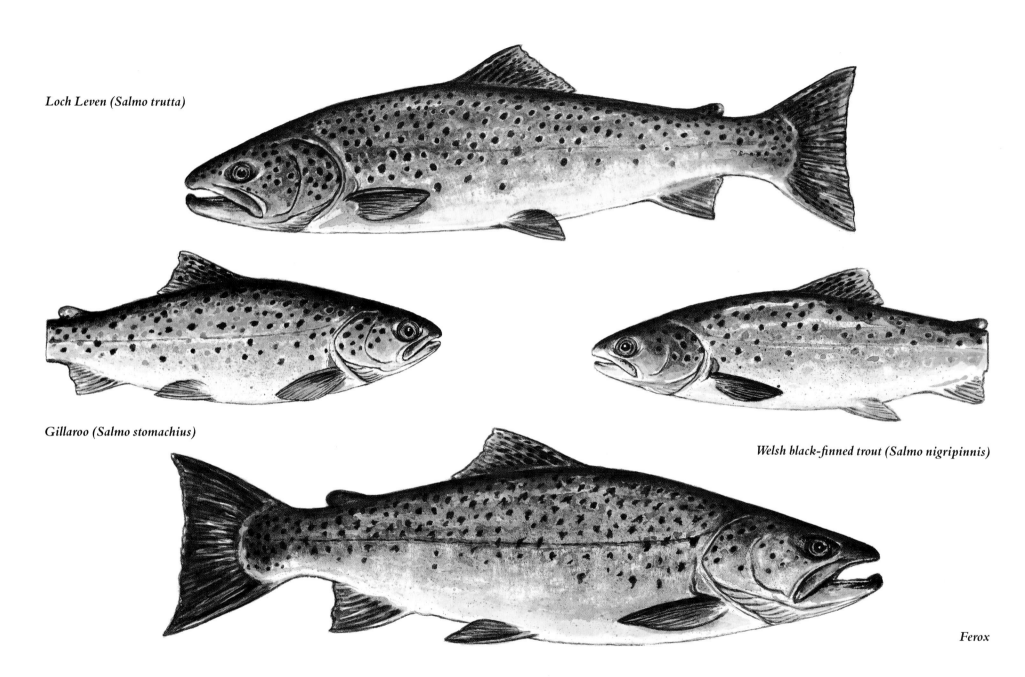

Loch Leven (Salmo trutta)

Gillaroo (Salmo stomachius)

Welsh black-finned trout (Salmo nigripinnis)

Ferox

macrostigma (the distinctively blotched trout of North Africa and Turkey) are probably descendants of those whose instinct led them to stay in the less warm waters of the region.

For many years it was thought that there were different species of brown trout, but it is now accepted there is only one. In 1864, Dr Albert Günther catalogued ten species for the British Isles alone, including the Galway seatrout (*S. gallivensis*) and the Welsh black-finned trout (*S. nigripinnis*). In 1886, H. G. Seeley identified 29 different types of trout. In recent years a technique of 'chemical fingerprinting' called electrophoresis has enabled scientists to investigate more closely the extent to which some of these subspecies are determined by genetic differences and which are the product of ecological conditions.

A special interest has been taken in the fish of Lough Melvin, on the border of Fermanagh and Leitrim in Ireland. Three visually quite distinct types of trout co-exist in this water, yet they do not interbreed: the sonaghan (the black-finned trout referred to above, a fish of dark silver flanks and bold black spots), the gillaroo or 'red fellow' (*S. stomachius*, so called because of its remarkably thick stomach walls, developed to cope with its diet of snails), and finally the 'ferox', an old brownie with a large head and an appetite for char. Yet these are all brown trout, even though they appear to have taken up residence in the lough quite separately, as the ice receded.

One other strain of brownie that merits description, because it has long been prized for stocking abroad, is the Loch Leven fish, a lithe, silvery creature without red spots. Its home water, by Kinross in Scotland, was the first venue for flyfishing competitions, and it is said to have derived its name from its eleven islands, eleven streams, eleven different fish, and the fact that its shores were owned by eleven different lairds. The internal anatomy of this fish is remarkable for the extra filamentous processes attached to its intestinal tract, which the unwary angler, gutting his catch, might take for a sign of infestation or malignant growth. In fact, the Loch Leven trout is accounted one of the best of all brown trout for the table.

With so many local variations, it is difficult to describe a 'typical' brown trout in terms of coloration. Physically, they are all teleosts, or bony fishes with skeletons, and they are quite a primitive fish. Three-fifths of their body is composed of long muscular flanks – which makes for good eating – encased in an armour of cycloid scales that grow like miniature fingernails. This in turn is covered by a skin of very thin, mucus-secreting cells which produce the slime that seals the scales against infection and lubricates the fish's body.

The trout has eight fins including the tail, which is forked when young but matures into a distinctive, square rudder. The true trout can be differentiated from char (both the 'brook trout' and 'lake trout' of North America are char) by a curious vestigial appendage called the adipose fin, a small wobbly fin just forward of the tail, the exact function of which is uncertain. They also have teeth all along the vomerine bone in the centre top of the mouth, whereas char display them only on the tip.

Brown trout are capable of growing to very large sizes, especially the lake variety known as the ferox

Everywhere they are distinguished by local variation in colour and profile

which is found across Europe and Scandinavia. Contrary to most angling lore, these are not catchable exclusively on deep-trolled baits, because they do at times venture into the shallows. The British record brown trout was a ferox of 39½ pounds, caught in Loch Awe in 1866 by a Mr Muir of Inistrynich. It was foul-hooked on a salmon-fly, took 2½ hours to land, was set up stuffed in a case, but later got destroyed in a fire. Several other massive contenders, such as the celebrated 'Pepper's Ghost', turned out to be landlocked salmon that had adopted a dark tartan livery.

The specific coloration of brown trout depends partly on its habitat; on the whole, however, a resident of peat-stained waters will be darker-skinned and therefore better camouflaged for its environment than a trout from a clear-water stream, which will have adapted by being paler and more golden. Skin colour is regulated by light entering the eye of the fish and sending messages via nerves to the cells that contain pigment. A blind fish is therefore often black or vulnerably pale.

The dorsal region of the trout contains chromatophores, tiny colour sacs holding yellow, black, red and orange pigment; there are also reflective tissues, or iridocytes, mainly in the ventral region, which are crystals that reflect pigment and account for the sheen. The trout has a pale belly which renders it less visible for attack from below, and a back of dark brown or green. Its flanks are susceptible to almost limitless variation, but comprise essentially dark spots on a lighter background which ranges from silver through gold to rich brown. Spotting may be large cruciform charcoal, or orange stipple, or vermilion flecks, and

the dark spots are sometimes framed in a paler halo. The hue of this livery changes with the time of year and the condition of the individual fish, and darkens noticeably toward spawning seasons.

To illustrate this splendid variety – surely one of the prime features to celebrate in the trout – I give two descriptions of the most attractive brownies I have ever encountered. Their habitats could scarcely be more different, representing the geographical extremes of British waters. The first come from the tiny River Thrushel in Devon, where, the last time I fished it, I caught eighteen in one afternoon; they rose like lightning to a tiny dryfly, and weighed about five to the pound, but on a 2-weight rod they gave a lively account of themselves. The back is dark olive, the flanks bronze with black spots and red pinpoints, the ventral fins edged lightly with chalky white, and the extremity of the tail tinged with the most delicate rose-pink. I cannot tell what the colour of their flesh was, because such exquisite creatures belong in the stream, not on the plate.

Up in the Outer Hebrides, on the craggy island of Harris where I spend my summers, my father-in-law has a loch that contains some trout of remarkable size for the region. Ownership of trout-fishing rights is a legal minefield in Scotland, but rights can be purchased and protected for migratory species, and Loch Plocrapool was once a well-known water for seatrout and salmon. Sadly, like so many systems in these far-flung parts of Britain, it has suffered badly from poaching of the outflow by indiscriminate netting. The native brownies remain, however, and are as good a match as any seatrout if only you can hook one.

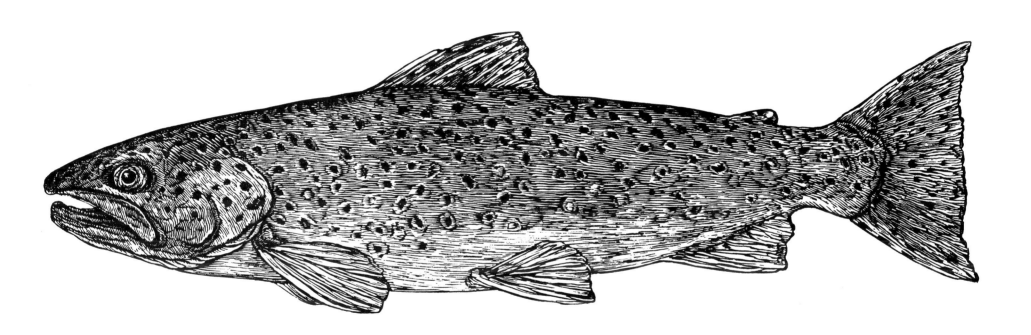

**Brown trout from a
highland burn**

The Hebrides have essentially two types of loch: the eutrophic, or fertile, *machair* lochs where acidity is not too high and the trout grow silvery and pink of flesh; and the bleaker peat lochs where available food is very scarce, and the natives may be no larger than fingerlings. There are dozens of lochs and lochans, though, and even those within a few hundred yards of each other may vary quite dramatically in terms of the trout they support. As well as being a spectacular place, with islets of bracken and rowan, cliffs and narrows and shallows and chasms, Plocrapool is known among the island's anglers as one of the premier venues for wild brownies. The fish are not free surface risers, but the feeding is rich – I suspect they subsist on a diet of sticklebacks and corixa – and they are butter-fat, with dark-yellow, black-splodged sides, short heads, and a curious bluish sheen. You seldom seem to catch one weighing less than a pound, and the family record is somewhat over four. A long vacation in early summer, perhaps with a small echo-sounder and a deep line, might one day reveal just how large these beauties really do grow.

One year we tried introducing a limited batch of rainbow trout from a trout-farm in Lewis, but the experiment was not a success. These fish, which have been extensively injected into European waters, are not at home in such an environment, and they failed to compete with the hardy native stock. The rainbow (*S. gairdneri*) is a native of the rivers of the Pacific seaboard of North America from the Bering Sea in Alaska to the south of California, its *locus classicus* being the Sacramento River. It is known as the kamloops in its lake form, the steelhead in its sea-going form, and also as

the silver trout; there is a group of subspecies called the golden trout (*S. aquabonita* for example, which can be taken by trekking above 10,000 feet in the High Sierras) which is about as highly coloured as any trout can get, with red cheeks, flanks of red, yellow and gold, and white tips to the dorsal and anal fins.

Although some of the specimens that are produced by British hatcheries are sorry versions of the real thing, the wild rainbow is a most eye-catching trout, in or out of the water. Its back is of a deep greenish blue and the silvery sides are marked with a pinkish or magenta ribbon that extends up the body either side of the lateral line. Apart from the pale belly, the fish is covered with a sprinkling of small black dots, including the head and fins and (unlike the brownie) the tail. Also unlike the brownie, which is more of an individualist, the rainbow has a touch of the dandy about it, an apparent air of confidence that can verge on the swaggering and prove its downfall. Smaller fish (especially those stocked in stillwaters) tend to shoal up together; when hooked, the rainbow frequently takes to the air in spectacular fashion, though he has not the dour stamina of the dogged brownie. They are indeed quite different in temperament.

Although certain waters, like the Armstrong in Montana, are now among the finest rainbow fisheries in the world, the introduction of this Pacific species was long resented by the traditional anglers of the last century who preferred the native American 'brookie' as a quarry. The precise date when the rainbow was transplanted to the Eastern States is not certain – various authorities place it as early as the 1870s – but it was widely settled by the end of the last century, and,

Rainbow (Salmo
gairdneri)

as we shall see, it also proved spectacularly successful in its expatriate roles.

Another native of the west (and probably, with the rainbow, an ancestor of the golden trout) is the cutthroat trout (*S. clarki*), which ranges in habitat from southern Alaska down to New Mexico but is not established in Europe. There are some ten subspecies of 'cutts', and they have been recorded at weights of at least 40 pounds (the biggest rainbow being a fish of 52½ pounds, from British Columbia), and they interbreed easily with the rainbow itself. This is another attractive and variegated trout, with silvery-orange flanks, an olive back, and dark spots. Its name is derived from the bright slashes of red across the throat under the gill-covers that make it look like one of Sweeney Todd's unfortunate victims.

Since, like the trout, they are members of the *Salmonidae* family, we should also consider two types of char that are native to North America, both of which are known colloquially as 'trout' and have been introduced to Europe. The 'brookie' is a native of the Atlantic streams and lakes of north-east America, and is extremely intolerant of warm water. As the result of ecological changes, such as deforestation, which raise the temperature of the water, it is now less widespread than it was, and large specimens are rare – anglers with access to floatplanes may seek out unmolested water-ways, or can pursue larger brookies in the Argentine where they have been introduced.

The brook trout is classified as *Salvelinus fontinalis*, and is also known as speckled trout, aurora trout and squaretail. Like all char, it has a leathery feel to its skin and its scales are tiny. It has a characteristic marbled appearance over its back, dorsal fin and tail, with pale spots ranging from lemon to buff, on a darker background. While it may also display red spots, the char has no dark ones, thus distinguishing it from the true trout. Its lower fins are edged in white, the anal fin showing a black stripe. It spawns in autumn, and at this time the male will turn quite red in his ventral region. Brookies have been tried out in Britain, without much permanent success, since 1869, but they are easily caught and do not reproduce in the wild. The same is true of those two curious hybrids, the tiger trout (brook × brown) and the cheetah trout (brook × rainbow), though they, too, are pretty to look at.

Common ancestry is shared between the brookie and another char indigenous to North America, the lake trout or *Salvelinus namaycush*. The laker, gray trout, togue or mackinaw is essentially a denizen of deep, cold lakes, though it can be found for a brief period in the littoral or marginal areas immediately after the winter ice disappears. It has a forked tail, a greenish body covered in pale vermicular markings, and specimens of 20–30 pounds are regularly caught trolling with metal lines and downriggers. The record remains a freak of 102 pounds caught in a net in Lake Athabaska, Saskatchewan, in 1961 (the brookie record, by comparison, is still held by Dr William Cook's fish of 14½ pounds, taken in 1916 from the Nipigon by Lake Superior), and it also thrives in some Alpine and Scandinavian lakes.

An important hybrid of the char is the wendigo, or splake, a fertile cross between the male brookie and the female laker, which retains the distinctive square tail of the brook trout. This has been successfully introduced

Brook trout (Salvelinus fontinalis)

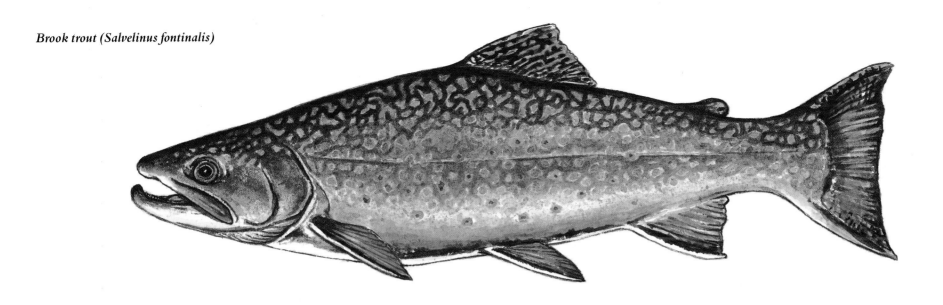

Char (Salvelinus alpinus)

Lake trout (Salvelinus namaycush)

into such waters as the Great Lakes, where native populations of trout have been destroyed by predation, and has proved highly adaptable to the existing ecosystem.

There are, of course, char native to Britain, but they are rarely of much consequence to the angler, since they tend to seek out the colder layers of water in the thermocline of the lakes, where they have become a landlocked species, and venture into the shallows only after dark. They are in fact more widely distributed than most people imagine, thriving in some 200 lochs and lakes. *Salvelinus alpinus* (or, as the French more elegantly put it, *omble-chevalier*) is a shoaling fish in fresh water that has developed several subspecies. It resembles a brownie in overall appearance, though the belly of the male has more of a lemon shade, the back has pale spots and the upper edges of the fins are fringed with white. The underside of the male becomes rubicund as the spawning season approaches, and this is the origin of its name, from the Gaelic *ceara*, red.

Char feed mainly on plankton and shrimp in stillwater, but they used to be caught in great numbers by professional fishermen trolling for them with deeply presented polished spinners on such waters as Lake Windermere; potted char, a paste composed of spices, butter and flesh, was a speciality of the Lake District. The only char I have ever caught was on a small wetfly in Sutherland's Loch Stack, a water once renowned for its large seatrout. Against all the odds, it happened during an August heatwave at midday in a flat calm, when the boat in which we were idling was suddenly surrounded by a shoal of dimpling fish; what they were taking we could not discover, but by chance I hooked a small char on a size-12 Alexandra, and I still remember how delicious its fine flesh tasted the next morning.

Before leaving our description of some of the trout after which anglers hanker, it is necessary to consider their sea-going varieties. All these trout are to a certain extent naturally migratory and, even in those populations that are stationary in waters cut off from the sea, they may display certain modified migratory instincts; stocked rainbows are notorious for slipping away downriver, lake trout in all countries tend to run up feeder streams to spawn, and resident brownies will move up even a pool or two later in the season.

In trout that migrate to sea it is not clear what the genetic factor is that revives the anadromous (ocean-going) instinct, or indeed whether such trout were originally marine species which began to seek the safer protection of fresh water for spawning, or freshwater stocks which began to venture out to sea for improved feeding. Metallic blue steelhead run the north-western American rivers, brookies revisit their streams as 'coasters', and the brown trout that goes to sea is known as a seatrout.

If we concentrate on the British seatrout as an example, it might be described as a trout aspiring to the condition of a salmon – and indeed fishmongers and restaurateurs often cash in on its close, if superficial resemblance to a small salmon by advertising it as a 'salmon trout', though in fact it starts out life as a trout pure and simple. While it is physiologically identical to the brown trout, its behaviour is so different that several writers deal with it as *Salmo trutta*

trutta, to distinguish it from the resident brownies. It is also known by a mass of other local names, depending on the size and season of its return to fresh water: finnock, peal, white trout, herling, sewin, scurf, truff, shigglers, whitling and black-tails.

It spawns in fresh water, and the parr are similar to those of the stationary browns; but after two or three years it turns silver, becomes a smolt (like a salmon) and drops down into salt water where it puts on weight rapidly, feeding off fish fry and sandeels. Many seatrout stay quite close to the coast, but others seem to stray as far as several hundred miles from the estuary. When they do ascend the rivers they are the most spectral, shy and elusive of all gamefish and, pound for pound, surely the best fighters among the salmonids. Seatrout are a veritable cult fish, and whole books have been written about how to catch them, the classic being by Hugh Falkus, Britain's foremost angling writer, who pioneered the bewitching practice of flyfishing for them at night.

A Gaelic proverb holds that there are but three creatures beautiful in death – a blackcock, a human child, and a seatrout. The latter, with his pelagic hues (dark back and silver sides), taken straight off the tide is a peerless trout, and many a salmon angler will lay down his heavier tackle and take up a single-handed rod for the incomparable experience of seeing the slim silver runner dance at his fly. These are not to be confused with ordinary brownies which drop down merely to the estuaries (slob, or bull trout) and which have red spots as well as a silvery sheen but which are altogether more flabby in texture.

Golden (Salmo aquabonita)

Cutthroat (Salmo clarki)

23

*Seatrout: the most
spectral, shy and elusive
of all gamefish*

THE HUMAN TOUCH
TROUT AND THEIR NEW HORIZONS

The trout is no single, common, identical, definite,
determined and measureable fish, but rather ten
thousand tantalizing, distinct and different devils.

Sir Charles J. Holmes: *THE TARN AND THE LAKE*

Although today some of the world's most prolific trout fishing is to be had in the southern hemisphere, neither rainbow nor brown is originally a native species there. The story of their arrival is a rather romantic one, a tribute to the determination of sportsmen and the resilience of the species. In fact, if we first consider the distribution away from Europe of the brown trout during the last century it makes one appreciate how this fish has truly become a citizen of the world.

It is a remarkable fact that all today's Antipodean brownies are descendants of an original consignment of 3,000 ova that arrived from Britain in 1864. After several unsuccessful attempts in 1852 and 1858 to transport salmon eggs, which were dispatched to Australia but died when they hatched too early en route, the legislature of Tasmania, anxious to stock their rivers, formed an Honorary Commission to oversee the project, and its supervisor in Britain was James Arundel Youl.

In the latter year, 50,000 salmon eggs packed in ice were sent aboard the steamer *Curling* from Liverpool, but they hatched after 59 days; two years later, another batch aboard the *Beautiful Star* met with a similar fate; but by this time Youl had realized that the ova had to be refrigerated at a temperature of between 33° and 35°F, and he arranged for his next consignment to be contained in an ice-house of 30 tons capacity, packed in wooden crates lined with charcoal, crushed ice and nests of moss. But at the last moment his supply of eyed salmon ova failed. A letter of appeal was published in *The Times*, and 90,000 salmon ova were quickly promised, along with the offer, from those two sterling piscicultural experts, Francis Francis and Frank Buckland, of 1,000 eyed brownie ova from the Itchen, and a further 2,000 from the little River

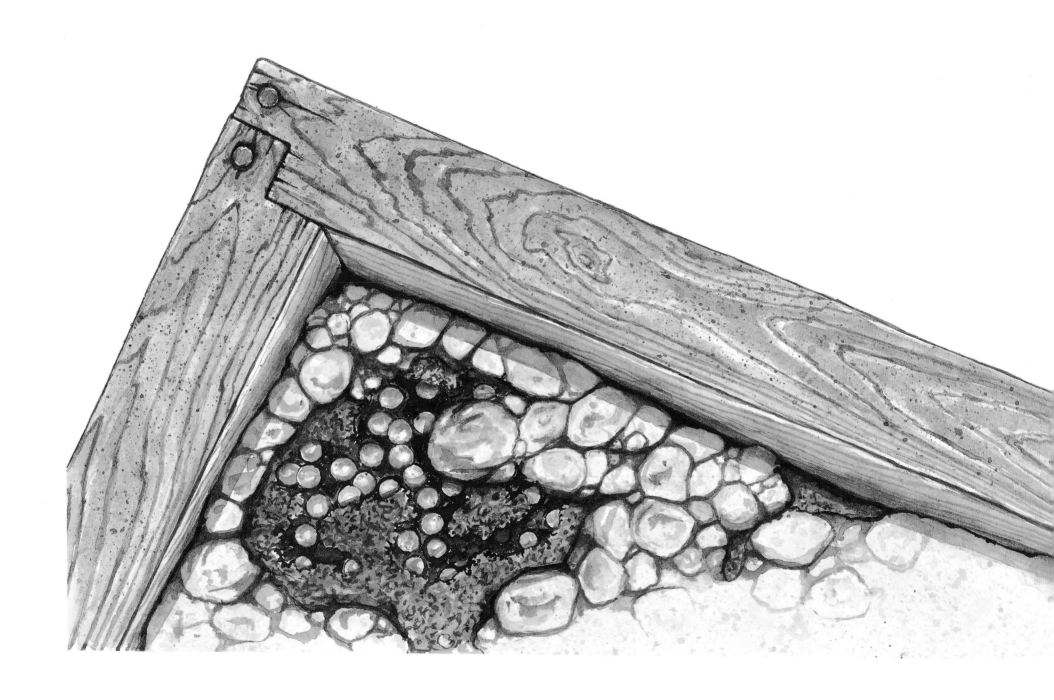

Wick, in Buckinghamshire. On 21 January 1864 this historic cargo sailed aboard the clipper *Norfolk* out of Falmouth, arriving at Melbourne on 15 April. The boxes were transferred to a sloop bound for Hobart, and were unloaded in Tasmania some 91 days after setting sail.

But 300 brown trout eggs had survived, and the first hatched on 4 May in that year. In 1866, 171 were thriving in the hatchery, and 38 were stocked into the Plenty River, where they spawned that July (being the Antipodean winter), while the rest were retained as brood stock. These provided the 800 eggs that were taken over to the South Island of New Zealand the following year, where they also thrived. The salmon, incidentally, appeared to do well initially and there was a show of grilse in the Derwent River in 1867, but they then disappeared. It was the fortuitous brownie that won the day.

The credit for introducing the brown trout to North America goes to Fred Mather, who visited the International Fisheries Exhibition in Berlin in 1880 and befriended Baron Lucius von Behr, President of the prestigious fishing association Deutscher Fischerei Verein. He sent some 80,000 ova from the trout in his Black Forest streams, and these arrived on a steamship in New York in February 1883; some of them were hatched at Cold Spring Harbour and others in Northville (Michigan) and were first stocked in the Pere Marquette River. These were not in fact the very first brown trout to hatch on that continent: in 1882, W. L. Gilbert of Plymouth (Massachusetts) had received a shipment of 4,000 ova, of which three hatched but were never planted out.

Ova in a shipping crate – cradle of these citizens of the world

The brownies soon acclimatized themselves and spread, augmented in 1884 by an influx of Loch Leven strain, and by 1900 they were established in some 38 States. But not everyone was happy with the newcomers, any more than they were with the rainbows when they switched coasts. The European fish were called 'German browns' and were regarded as interlopers which gobbled up fry and chased away the much easier to catch brookies – though their arrival was in fact timely, considering the threat that was already upon the native char from depredations on its environment.

So well did the brownies do in their new land of opportunity that it was from here rather than Europe that they were exported to Japan in 1892, where they were introduced to Lake Chuzenji. The Japanese now have four varieties of trout, and are responsible for some of the most ingenious and competitively priced trout tackle on the market; and they have a long tradition of angling enthusiasm. Ebisu – one of their seven Gods of Fortune – is a smiling figure holding a fishing rod in his hand and with a plump *tai*, or red bream, tucked under his left arm. Since ancient times, Japanese nobles have fished for tiny species from lakeside temples constructed for the purpose, sometimes using lines made of a single human hair; and one especially philosophical sage would never even use a bait, lest in catching a fish he interrupted his enjoyment of the process of anticipation and reflection. Today, pressure being what it is, Japanese trout fanatics charter helicopters in New Zealand to take them to the unspoiled streams that could previously be reached only after days of hard slog. If they are denied

'German' brown and rainbow. Not everyone was happy with the newcomers

this, there is always the opportunity at home of casting for trout in the municipal swimming-pools, where they are stocked in the autumn. One feels that this noble fish deserves better.

So great was the demand for the brownie as a sporting trophy during the heyday of the British Empire that it became almost as much of a colonial trademark as the *chota peg* and the flywhisk. It was successfully introduced to the rivers of Natal in 1890 and to the Cape Province of South Africa in 1892, after seventeen years of failure. Ova from Loch Leven as well as German sources were imported into Kenya in 1905 at the personal expense of Major Ewart Grogan; these ancestors of the stocks now established high up in the Aberdare Mountains had to survive a sea-journey of 7,000 miles, a further 400 by train, and then a shaky ride carried on the heads of bearers, before they reached the hatchery.

The governing forces of the Raj in India had to wait until 1900 before the solution to the almost insuperable problems of refrigeration and transport led to a successful stocking of trout in Kashmir, their favoured summer retreat. The Duke of Bedford sent several batches of ova to his friend the Maharajah, and perhaps it was a scion of one of these aristocratic gifts which graced my own honeymoon. Brownies are to be found today across Africa and Asia, and they were shipped extensively to South America, where some of the finest wild fishing for them is now to be found. They arrived in Argentina in 1904, in Chile in 1905 and in Peru in 1928, and they exist as far south as Tierra del Fuego. They were introduced to the Falkland Islands after the Second World War and since 1947 have established a lively sea-going run.

By comparison, the rainbow trout has had a more revolutionary effect on the popularity of angling as a sport in recent years because it is also reared extensively as a fish for the table. But the little trout in its clingfilm convenience on the shelves of the supermarket, and the often disgracefully flaccid 'pink trout' one encounters in restaurants which has been cooked to disintegration point under a sprinkling of almonds, is not the type of rainbow one wishes to celebrate. Yet without this ancillary market it is doubtful whether the angler – in Europe at least – would enjoy such a wide choice of trout-stocked rivers to fish.

The rainbow was first imported into Britain in 1885 and reared in the Howietoun hatchery of Sir James Maitland, whence the Loch Leven browns had departed for America the previous year. These were of the *Salmo shasta* strain from the Sierra Nevada, a winter-spawning rainbow; but the sad fact is that this brilliant and most welcome trout has never been capable of breeding widely in the wild over here. In the Derbyshire Wye and the Buckinghamshire Chess they do reproduce, and also in the lovely little Misbourne in Buckinghamshire, which is the only place in Britain where I have seen them on the redds.

Thanks to the generosity of one of my fishing companions, several times each year I am able to visit the delightfully appointed lake which he owns near Amersham, and here flourishes a stock of self-supporting brown and rainbow trout that, I believe, is unrivalled as a mixed wild fishery anywhere in the country. The water is crystalline, though prone to heavy weed growth in the summer months, being eutrophic, and you can work your way down the little river into the mouth of the lake in a punt and see the pockets of wild rainbow trout clustered below you as you cast. There is no confusing one of these freshwater daemons for a fish that has spent its earlier days with its nose hard up against a hatchery grille, for they take off like a salmon when you set the hook. They are also somewhat longer in the head than most stew-fed rainbows, and both the crimson stripe and the background coloration are noticeably darker. They are rare prizes indeed.

The rainbow has proved an ideal fish for rearing because it grows more quickly than the brown, and, though its life is shorter, it is a better bet for those operating the many commercial 'put-and-take' waters that are now the staple fare of many an English flyfisher's diet. Rainbows are also more tolerant of warmer water (though, being thermotropic, like all trout, they cannot cope with sudden rises in temperature), which means they will offer sport during the summer months when, especially in our still waters, the brownie tends to disappear into deeper holes and skulk there until autumn.

Stocked into many of the hallowed chalk-streams that were once the exclusive preserves of the native brownie, the rainbow is on the whole a blessing, even if it does compete very successfully for food and space, because it is generally a containable presence – except where unwelcome numbers of small fish escape from hatcheries and become a pest. They have also taken well in our larger reservoirs, where the space and variety of available food allows them to mend the often mildewed and fin-ragged condition in which

some suppliers still deliver them; and they overwinter in large numbers, such 'residuals' being in fine fighting form earlier in the spring than the brownies, and showing a good conversion rate of food to weight.

The problem that rainbows have, of losing their condition and becoming lank and dark as they go into spawning livery but being unable to shed eggs or milt, is now less common than it was. Interbreeding has produced a variety of strains so that, at any given time of the year, a fishery manager should be able to acquire trout that are in the peak of condition; there is also a variety known as the 'triploid' that does not undergo a spawning transformation at all. Since it is in practice an almost entirely artificial presence in this country, in many places there is no close season for the rainbow; and, while this is good news for anglers intent on casting a line every day of the year, it is not a very good policy for the overall well-being of a public-access fishery to allow fishing to continue uninterrupted throughout the calendar. Even if the resident stock is being removed and replaced on a fairly brisk basis, the banks and vegetation need a rest if the environment is not to be reduced to a muddy hole in the ground (and there are plenty of those around and, seemingly, enough anglers sufficiently indifferent to the quality of their surroundings to make such venues profitable). A rainbow dragged from such a place is rarely a fish of much beauty, and I for one can think of few reasons for catching a fish that one does not admire; but many anglers think that fishing for them is preferable to not fishing at all, and I suppose they are entitled to their opinion.

If a definite improvement in the overall quality of

the stocked rainbow has been seen during the last fifteen years, it is largely due to the practice of selective breeding. One of the pioneers of this admirable and sensible process was the late Sam Holland, who established in the 1970s at his Avington fishery in Hampshire a strain of rainbow he rather cheekily called 'supertrout'. What he did, quite simply, was to reverse the usual tendency of the farmer to sell off the fastest-growing fish first and to retain the weaker and slower members of the batch for the following year's brood stock. Instead, he separated those which developed most quickly, and bred from them progressively until he was able to bring on young fish of much higher average weights and – most important in terms of prestige for his fishery – rainbow trout that could be brought on to previously unheard-of weights which

they would never have attained in their short lifetimes.

Other fish farmers were quick to see the market potential for rainbows of this size, and followed suit. In the event, it has led to an altogether undesirable competition: to stick the biggest possible waddling stockfish into a confined area for the express purpose of its being extracted as rapidly as possible and pictures of its corpse being spread across the pages of the angling press. This is not quite the same thing as breeding a champion racehorse or a prize bull, but the fault lies not with the breeders so much as with those anglers who measure their achievements in life by absolute, rather than relative, details. If nothing else, it has proved the potential of *Salmo gairdneri* in this country, and the fisherman's year would be considerably poorer without its presence.

Brown trout chasing a mayfly

*Selective breeding can
produce rainbows of
tremendous proportions*

SCIMITAR OF LIGHT
HABITAT, DANGERS AND LIFE-CYCLE

He hangs, a scimitar of light,
Miraculously in our sight,
Giving one moment to observe
His brief but agitated curve.

Robert Bell: *THE TROUT*

To thrive, trout need clean, well-oxygenated water that provides food, shelter, and reaches where they can reproduce. It is perhaps surprising that there are so many places in the modern world where these requirements are still met.

Fast, cool streams suit them very well: rough water contains more dissolved oxygen than calm water, since it offers a greater surface area to the atmosphere. In still waters, trout need the symbiotic presence of weeds and other underwater vegetation, because plants in sunlight give out oxygen as the byproduct of photosynthesis. (This process is of course reversed at night, when they produce carbon dioxide. It is for this reason that circumspect nurses remove flowers from the bedside at the end of the day, or so the story goes.) Trout are capable of surviving in water beneath ice, but if the ice is overlaid with snow that blocks out the sunlight, they will suffocate because the plant life in the water can no longer provide them with oxygen.

At either end of their range of temperature tolerance (which varies from species to species) trout become torpid; in warm weather they require more oxygen for their metabolism, yet warm water contains less oxygen in solution. Both plants and currents are therefore crucial for survival, and the fish will shift habitat, where possible, to compensate for adverse changes in conditions.

Plant life also forms a crucial part of the whole 'food web' under water, for algae and phytoplankton are minute examples of the vegetable kingdom on which feed in turn the larvae, fry and crustacea that in the end support the trout itself. Without what one might call this powerbase there would not exist the minnows and shrimps, mayflies and other aquatic bugs on which the fish batten daily. It has been suggested that, at every stage of this web or chain, it requires ten pounds

Rainbow coming to a pupa

of food to produce a pound of its predator, and since the trout is up at the very top of this pecking order it obviously relies on a healthy support system beneath it.

Phytoplankton need a supply of mineral salts, and so do algae. The most fertile trout waters are therefore those that are hard, or alkaline, where the water has washed in over soft rocks such as chalk or limestone and carried away a high proportion of minerals. Carbonates are especially important in speeding up photosynthesis, and calcium is crucial as a substance to be absorbed for the making of bones, and where there are rich levels of absorption of these substances there will be excellent potential for trout populations.

Of this precise kind are the spring-fed rivers, of which the most famous in the world are probably the chalk-streams of southern England. The chalk deposits, running in a band from Normandy through Hampshire and up to Yorkshire and surfacing in places, act like huge reservoirs which filter the rain and allow it to seep through into the rivers via what are known as aquifers, furnishing them with a constant and usually level supply of winter-stored water throughout the spring and summer.

Such waters are fortunate in two respects: they have a relatively high pH value, and they do not suffer from perilous fluctuations in flow. The pH value of water is measured on a scale of 1–14, with pH 7 being neutral, or that of distilled water. Anything below 7 is acidic; but the actual value will change slightly during the course of any twenty-four-hour period, being for instance more alkaline in the daytime when there is more oxygen available from plants. A steady flow also ensures the stability of both the plant life and the animal life of the system, a condition which is constantly threatened by modern developments in drainage, logging, canals, abstraction, dams, strip-mines and hydro-electric schemes.

The rain-fed streams are by contrast more susceptible to damaging extremes that may bring unacceptably high temperatures in summer, especially if the watertable is being tapped for other purposes and the current is reduced, and violent floods after winter thaws – plants, animal life and protective cover being scoured from the bed by the weight of water, ice or rock. In many cases, they are also those streams which have soft or acidic water in the first place, running in over rock such as granite that yields little in the way of mineral salts, and they can least afford to suffer. In such cases the population of native trout may be numerous, but they will tend to be small in size.

The nature of the river bottom is also important in this respect, as the fish prefer the gravel of chalk-streams or the silt of limestone rivers to muddy or sandy bottoms, where neither weeds nor incipient insect life can gain much purchase. With such precise requirements, the last thing they need on top of all this is the wholesale sabotage caused by short-sighted human activities.

Even in those rare places where the temperature and flow have not been unnaturally affected by the factors enumerated above, there is now the omnipresent threat of chemical pollution. Acid rain is a phenomenon so dangerous in Europe that it now looks positively apocalyptic. It was not until the nuclear reactor disaster at Chernobyl that most of the lay population came to understand that the future is no more predictable than the weather; but the circulation of cloud-systems bearing toxic chemicals has been quietly affecting our quality of life, if not our standard of living, for some decades. Acid rain encompasses the fallout from the skies (whether it is actually raining or not) of byproducts of fossil-fuel combustion and other industrial processes. These accumulate in the clouds and circulate far away from the places where they were initially produced, forming nitric and sulphuric acids that subsequently fall to earth and are absorbed into the soil, and eventually into the water. By leaching the precious alkali from both, acid rain is a progressive killer.

And so, too, is detergent that has been insufficiently processed by sewage plants before its release into rivers, for this product reduces the available oxygen in the water. Most of us in the Western world have developed out of necessity a blind faith in purification systems – especially when it comes to our drinking water – but it is curious what gets through the chinks. Just downstream from a sewage purification plant on the beat I fish for Tweed salmon each autumn there is evidence of another type of plant: the margins abound in seasonal crops of tomatoes which have been established from seeds passing through the works upstream. They are said to be perfectly edible – but it makes you wonder what other, less visible stuff is being merrily pumped into the current.

The wholesale release of toxic waste from factories – and even from fish-farms – is another hazard, as are the increasingly common seepages of chemical fertilizers and pesticides; the former can unbalance a pond or stream by choking it with accelerated vegetation, while the latter can of course exterminate certain areas of insect life. There is now much more that needs to be done to protect our waters than at any time since the worst excesses of the Industrial Revolution, and such dedicated bodies as the Anglers' Co-operative Association in Britain, and Trout Unlimited in North America deserve the support of any fisherman who would rather see his grandchildren catching a fish than having to rely on his hoary recollections about what a wild trout used to look like.

With the exception of those sea-going varieties that have already been mentioned, the life-cycle of most trout is much the same, the two main variables being longevity and the seasons for spawning. In places like New Zealand's Lake Taupo and the Great Lakes of North America, there are massive annual migrations of trout from the stillwaters, running the streams and rivers where they will spawn, and these afford the angler some opportunities for brisk sport. We shall go on to consider the life of the brown trout as a representative role-model.

The male matures at two to three years of age; as spawning time approaches his skin darkens and he develops a neb or kype, a distinctive hooked ending to his jaws. The female does not generally mature until she is a year older, which allows her some extra time for putting on size and weight. The timing of spawning preparation depends on the nature of the particular water; in colder habitats, where the eggs will take longer to hatch and the parent fish will take longer to regain condition, trout may be moving up into position towards the end of September, whereas in

Hawthorn fly (Bibio marei)

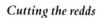

Cutting the redds

more clement places they do not spawn until the New Year (I am speaking here of the months relevant to the northern hemisphere).

Brownies like to spawn on clean gravel in brisk, well-aerated streams where the temperature is between 41° and 55°F. They avoid areas with excessive silt, which stifles the eggs. Cutting the redds (as the spawning beds are called) is performed by the female: she turns on her side above the gravel, her ventral fins spread for balance, and with vigorous, spring-like convulsions of her body aquablasts a nest a few inches deep with the sweeps of her tail. She does not use the tail to scoop the gravel directly, though that is how it appears. Her suitor is meanwhile hovering near by, and is poised to defend his nuptial bed against other males, whom he chases off to the best of his ability.

When the nest is ready, both fish lie close over the trench, their taut bodies often touching, and the eggs and milt are released simultaneously. The female tilts up, her mouth open, while both fish shudder in a paroxysm of what looks like ecstasy and relief. At this stage, one of the lingering rivals will sometimes dash in and ejaculate his own milt, a way of guarding against infertility in a batch. The eggs sink and are covered over by the female with gravel from the next cutting as she works her way upstream until she is spent. This may take a couple of days, depending on her size and the total number of eggs – from a few hundred in a small fish up to several thousand.

The sperm goes straight to work, and those which fail to penetrate an egg die within one minute. Overall time from fertilization to hatching varies immensely with temperature; at a regular 50°F it would take about

one month, whereas in icebound rivers it can take as long as five months. Half-way through incubation (on average, three to four weeks) the pulse and distinctive black eye of the embryo can be seen to have developed inside its globular capsule; and at the end of the incubation period it emerges as an alevin. These are curious-looking little beasts, about half an inch long, with soup-plate eyes and a cumbersome yolk-sac off which they feed for the first fortnight of their lives, skulking in the gravel of their nursery for safety until the drip-feed sustenance in their sacs is exhausted.

When they are about one inch in length, they begin to venture forth and feed on minute larvae and plankton. At this stage they are known as fry, and they begin to grow protective scales – like most animals, the trout comes naked into this world. Now starts a lifelong battle for the survival of the fittest, and infant mortality is horrifyingly high – up to ninety per cent in the first four months. Other fish and many birds are partial to a mouthful of fry, and many are simply too weak to find enough food for themselves amid the dense population. But in order merely to maintain the level of stocks (that is, zero rate of growth), each female during her lifetime need have only two eggs that make it to maturity; in most places, a couple in every batch of a thousand will probably survive to become adults.

At one year old, when the trout is three to four inches long, it is called a fingerling, or yearling; it should be double that length by the end of the next year, though of course this depends on the available food. The brownie takes about three years to build its weight up to a pound in the wild, and it is at its best

Stonefly (Plecoptera microcephala)

between three and four years. Although they can live for twice as long as rainbows, brownies are slower-growing; and their old age is often not a dignified one, since they go out of condition and find it hard to maintain body weight. Many of these older fish turn to cannibalism – the ferox is especially adept at surviving to a ripe age by this practice – but others grow lank and hook-jawed, and it is often better to remove them from the fishery.

The rainbow by comparison is generally a spring spawner, the females cutting their redds between March and May, although some runs of steelhead during the winter are already about to spawn and do not seem to require the warmer water. Fanatical anglers fishing for them often put themselves in danger of hypothermia, and in some regions the risk is so great that they are forbidden to fish unless in the company of another. They should perhaps heed the maxim of the Victorian angler who recommended inspecting one's legs beneath the waders every so often, and advised coming out of the water altogether for a spell once they had turned black.

Brown trout spawning

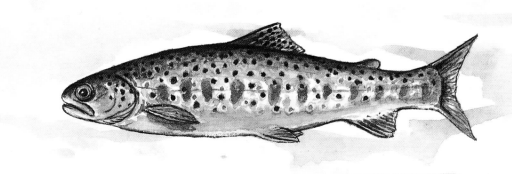

Life-cycle – ova, alevin, fry, parr

The Trout in its Element
Movement, Survival and the Senses

His bliss is older than the sun.
Silent and straight the waters run.
The lights, the cries, the willows dim,
And the dark tide are one with him.

Rupert Brooke: *THE FISH*

To be honest, we still know precious little about life under water; but this element is the fascinating catalyst in the entire angling process, and the idea of 'reading the water' bears tribute to this notion that each river and stream (and stillwater, to a lesser extent) has its own moods and personality and, some would claim, its own choreography and voice, too. Anglers are drawn irresistibly to water of almost any kind; they peer into it, try to guess where the lies, if any, might be, and scan the surface for signs of feeding fish. If they have any sense, they will also listen to it, getting an impression of its rhythm and flow. You only have to listen to Schubert's quintet, *Die Forelle* ('The Trout'), composed in 1819, to hear this process in reverse – music aspiring to the condition of water.

Though anglers sometimes have a vested interest in pretending otherwise, their precious trout are of rather a low order of intelligence. What passes for sheer cussedness and wiliness on the part of a fish which is being deliberately uncooperative or which has taken up a position in the current where eddies and drag make it quite impossible to present a dry-fly is not a sign of intelligence so much as the fish's well-developed sense of self-preservation, one of the reasons why it is so successful at maintaining so many thriving populations in a global variety of habitat.

I am often amazed at how some anglers, otherwise quite experienced, seem to be ignorant – or, at least, to ignore – when it comes to scaring trout. This is often the product of over-enthusiasm, and is a legacy that afflicts many city-dwellers who are forced to spend most of their days dodging traffic rather than looking up at the sky or considering the state of the wind. When they have a rare day at the water, they hurry down in order to get in that first, magical cast which always goes out with such relief and hope. But the best

.hing to do on approaching any trout water is to stop well short of it, and *look*.

It's no use spooking trout before you ever get to fish for them – but how often does this in fact happen, without our ever knowing there was a fish there in the first place? Watch a really seasoned trout angler: he will approach the water, prepared to cast over the nearest part first. He keeps low to the ground (some scoff at what they call his commando tactics, but that won't worry him in the least), having previously taken the very simple precaution of checking that the position of the sun will not announce his arrival by a creeping shadow long before he is within range of any potential quarry. He will attempt to minimize all vibration he may make as he moves, as any sensible hunter will when stalking anything. There is much to

be said for Robert Burton's dictum from his *Anatomy of Melancholy* (1621) that, 'Fishing is a kind of hunting by water.'

Contrast the more common behaviour of the angler who foolishly believes that the trout won't be aware of *him* until he can see the fish, at the earliest. On some of our larger stillwaters, especially, I frequently observe men weighed down with spare rods and other bulky clobber, striding straight up to their chosen area of bank, noisily dumping their impedimenta close to the water, unhooking their lure from the keeper-ring and plunging out into the lake to the limit of their wader-tops. What about the trout lurking in the margins, a particularly likely spot first thing in the morning? And, had there been some unobtrusively feeding there before the arrival of this automaton, what will have

Brookie with his eye on a muddler minnow

43

been the effect on other stocks – those same ones over whom our energetic friend is hoping to cast, as they dart away in panic? Why, they will all take fright and head off for somewhere quieter, leaving the angler to complain about the lack of a decent stocking-policy, no doubt.

The margins of some of our lakes and reservoirs are also devoid of fish because the subaquatic vegetation has been trampled down by these constant waders and now harbours no insect life to tempt the trout in close in the first place. Even on smaller waters, still and flowing, it is worth assuming that there will be a fish right under your rod-tip, first time over a stretch; like many other fishermen, I have hooked good trout when lying on my stomach with only the fly and nylon hanging down from the rod-tip, as well as by lowering baits and flies from a perch in a tree. If you're going to

Fish often lie under your rod-tip – they are not all under the far bank

opt for antics such as these (and there's no doubt they can put a trout in a creel on an otherwise difficult day), then it's as well to dress sensibly for the fray. Drab, even camouflaged clothing, may help break up your silhouette, although there is an argument for wearing a pale shirt if you are going to be standing exposed against a bright sky.

This basic precaution is nothing new – as was never more evocatively expressed than in Conrad Heresbach's *The Whole Art of Husbandry* (translated from the Latin in 1631): 'For as the fish is of a most pure sight, so they are of a most nice conceit, and where they once take offence, no flatterie can reconcile them: therfore his apparrell must be sad and deepe coloured like the water, plaine and close to his Bodie, and indeede so like a Shadow that it will give no shaddow.'

One further caveat. Most of today's commercially made rods come finished with a coat of glossy varnish, the main function of which is to impress the angler by its smooth sheen when handled in the tackle shop. Some manufacturers also fit golden rod rings and other such Rolls Royce options. But if you watch someone flycasting in bright weather from a distance you will notice a heliograph effect, whereby this varnished surface flashes brilliantly in the sun. We can only assume that a fish, which is wary above all things of strange and sudden movements above the water, will be put on its guard.

If you examine a trout's brain, you will notice that the two most pronounced features are the twin optical lobes and the large cerebellum; this tells us that nature has equipped the fish with the chief priorities of vision and movement. It hardly needs me to praise the agility of trout in water; and any angler watching a trout go for a fly will appreciate that it is particularly nimble in turning. The tissues and organs of the fish make it heavier than water, but it adjusts its buoyancy by means of regulating the air that it contains in its swim-bladder (this is crucial for the anadromous varieties in compensating for the more buoyant saline water). The functions of its eight fins are divided between stability and propulsion, and the precise hydrodynamics of this combination are very complex; but it has been shown that the trout moves by using its entire body, not just the fins, contorting it into a 'C' or 'S' shape and springing through the water.

In certain drastic experiments in which anaesthetized trout had all their fins amputated, scientists found that the fish could still swim tolerably well against currents. A trout can swim ten times its body-length per second when necessary, and is capable, for microseconds, of an accelerative rate equal to six times the force of gravity. Fortunately for the angler, this is not its normal rate of progress; but when anglers complain (especially in lakes) of being broken by 'smash takes' they are often wrong in attributing them to huge fish. Lake trout often feed at greater speed than we imagine, moving upwind and sipping in insects during a hatch; if they take your fly while moving directly away from you, and you tighten even briefly, a break is quite common, especially when using fine nylon and an imitative pattern.

There are two major, and two minor, functions of the fish's mouth. The first is obviously for feeding, which we shall examine in the next chapter; but it is worth considering here the question of whether trout have a sense of taste. There are taste buds in the mouth, and some over the surface of the body, but a trout does not chew its food and it does not seem to have a highly developed sense of taste if compared to a fish like the carp, which is so choosy that anglers have to keep coming up with tasty new baits almost every time they go to the water – composite carp baits available in Britain (where angling for this species probably includes the most intensely dedicated fishermen to be found anywhere) include 'boilies' flavoured with ox-blood, Pina Colada, and all kinds of fruit and cheese.

Trout do seem to prefer the taste of certain insects to others, because during a multiple hatch they can be quite selective in concentrating their attentions upon one species in particular – something very frustrating to the angler. The other minor function of the mouth –

which may, however, be of paramount importance for the angler – is that the trout is an inquisitive fish and, lacking hands, will use its mouth to investigate any unusual object which has excited its interest. We will see later how this can be exploited by the ingenious fisherman.

Respiration is the second major function of the mouth. Perhaps one of the most restful sights for anyone who loves to observe the delicate machinery of a trout's living body is the vision of it breathing gently in its native element. In running water, the fish will face upstream (though of course in the contraflow of a backwater or eddy it may be actually facing down-river) and appears to be gently gulping water into its mouth, while simultaneously ejecting it from the gills. This happens about fifty times every minute, and has a lovely rhythm to it.

The heart of the trout is directly behind its mouth (which is why, incidentally, fish that have gorged a bait seldom recover), and blood is pumped to the four pairs of gills, which are covered by a flap called the operculum. As water from the mouth passes through the gill arches, the blood in the gill filaments releases carbon dioxide and enriches itself by absorbing the oxygen dissolved in the water. The gill system of the fish is very delicate and should never be touched if the trout is to be released alive.

The question of the faculty of smell in the trout is difficult to resolve. Certainly they have little nostrils and nasal sacs, but these are not connected to the mouth as they are in the human. The olfactory sense remains something of a mystery; some anglers are assiduous in washing their hands before handling any bait and believe that odours such as sweat or tobacco can deter the trout. Also, there are on the market chemical extracts of chairomone and pheromone – the same substances that are said to be effective in sprays sold to men for secretly exuding an irresistible attraction for women – but it is doubtful whether, despite their popularity in some circles, they can be proved to work.

To return to our incautious angler at the beginning of this chapter; did he scare the fish before they saw him because they *heard* him, perhaps? And what of the old adage, perpetuated by anglers when beset by children on the bank, that you have to keep your voice down? Trout do in fact have ears, two internal ones with semicircular canals; but these, like our own inner ears, are more to do with maintaining equilibrium than for auditory purposes. Trout do not have the elaborate external cochlea of land animals; nor do they seem to be disturbed by noises in the air – gunshots or screaming jet-planes will not distract the trout from going about his quiet business. For centuries people were convinced that this was not the case, and that it was only a question of finding the right pitch to lure the trout to your net or spear – the fifty-ninth patent ever issued in England was for a 'fish-call'; and I have certainly seen a salmon-angler who had some faith in his salmon-whistle. After the hip-flask has been drained, anything seems possible.

What the trout *is* extremely sensitive to, however, is vibration that is transmitted through the water. Only fish and some amphibians possess what is known as a lateral line, a rather mysterious canal that runs – rather like the metal strip in a bank-note – the length of the

The delicate machinery of a trout's body

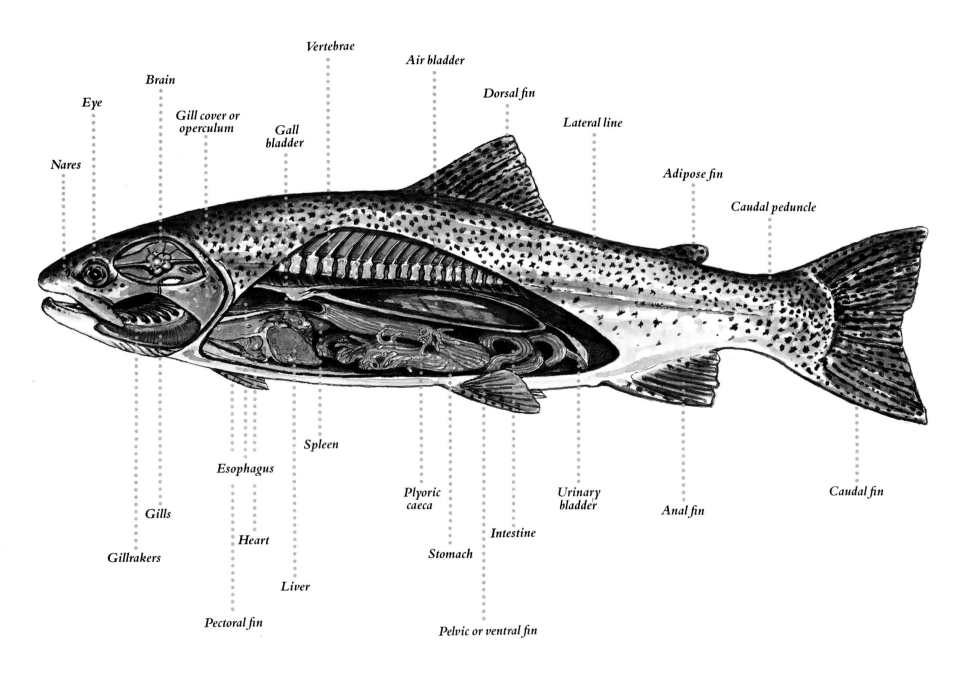

Nares

Eye

Brain

Gill cover or
operculum

Gall
bladder

Vertebrae

Air bladder

Dorsal fin

Lateral line

Adipose fin

Caudal peduncle

Gillrakers

Gills

Esophagus

Heart

Pectoral fin

Liver

Spleen

Plyoric
caeca

Stomach

Pelvic or ventral fin

Intestine

Urinary
bladder

Anal fin

Caudal fin

body, mid-way, and disappears either side of the head. This canal is filled with mucus and, when vibrations in the water are detected, the pressure on the mucus is relayed to sense-organs called ampullae which communicate them to the spinal cord. The usual analogy made is with a type of sonar system; but it is perhaps better not to think of it as an organ of hearing at all, but as a system of remote-control *touch*. It enables the trout to observe when danger – in the form of unfamiliar vibrations – may be approaching, but is also useful for navigating under murky conditions, and it is also sensitive to changes in temperature.

Trout hunt out their food mainly by sight, but the attractive vibrations of certain food items such as crippled baitfish, mice or frogs can help them to home in on some prey. Even primitive fishermen have known for centuries that shoals of sea-fish can be drawn to a particular spot by the judicious vibrating of poles or by splashing the surface with paddles to simulate the thrashing of shoals of smaller fish. Bill-fishermen often use a teaser that attracts the fish to the surface by wobbling and shaking, so that the lure proper will be inspected; and almost anyone who spins for predatory species is capitalizing on the fish's known responsiveness to vibrations felt along the lateral line.

The eye of the trout is not entirely dissimilar to the human eye, but there are two main differences when assessing its vision. First, because the refractive index of water is greater than that of air, light rays get bent as they pass from one medium to the other. Also, water has a tendency to absorb and disperse light-rays. The trout has a large eyeball that is filled with a transparent jelly, called vitreous humour, and an almost spherical lens, slightly flattened at the front, which protrudes through the iris. Light coming through the pupil of the iris (which has a fixed aperture, unlike that in man) is focused by the lens on to the retina, the dark blob that you can see if you peer into its eye.

The retina is often compared to the sensitive film in a camera, and it is composed of rods and cones connected to the optic lobes. Because the iris is fixed, changes in light intensity are accommodated by the rearranging of the retinal cells; but this takes a little time, with the result that the trout does not see well in sudden sunlight. It has one distinctive focusing muscle, the *retractor lentis*, which adjusts the distance between lens and retina in accordance with the distance of vision required. In their world, trout are not short-sighted, as is still sometimes supposed, nor are they colour-blind, although it is unlikely that they apprehend the same spectrum as we do, and certain ultra-violet colours may be more visible at certain depths.

The trout has a wide angle of vision in two lateral fields to either side of him under water, each of these seen by one eye only. For a limited angle directly ahead, he enjoys binocular vision, and there is a blind spot behind, which is considerably smaller than many people imagine, but is of vital use for the angler intent on sneaking up undetected. When the trout looks up, he sees in effect a clear window into the air, surrounded by a mirror that reflects back the bottom of the lake or stream. This is called Snell's Window, and may be imagined as an inverted cone with an angle of some 97°, at the bottom of which is the eye. The width

The trout has a wide angle of vision in two lateral fields to either side of him under water – for a limited angle directly ahead, he also enjoys binocular vision. Above, he sees through a window surrounded by a mirror

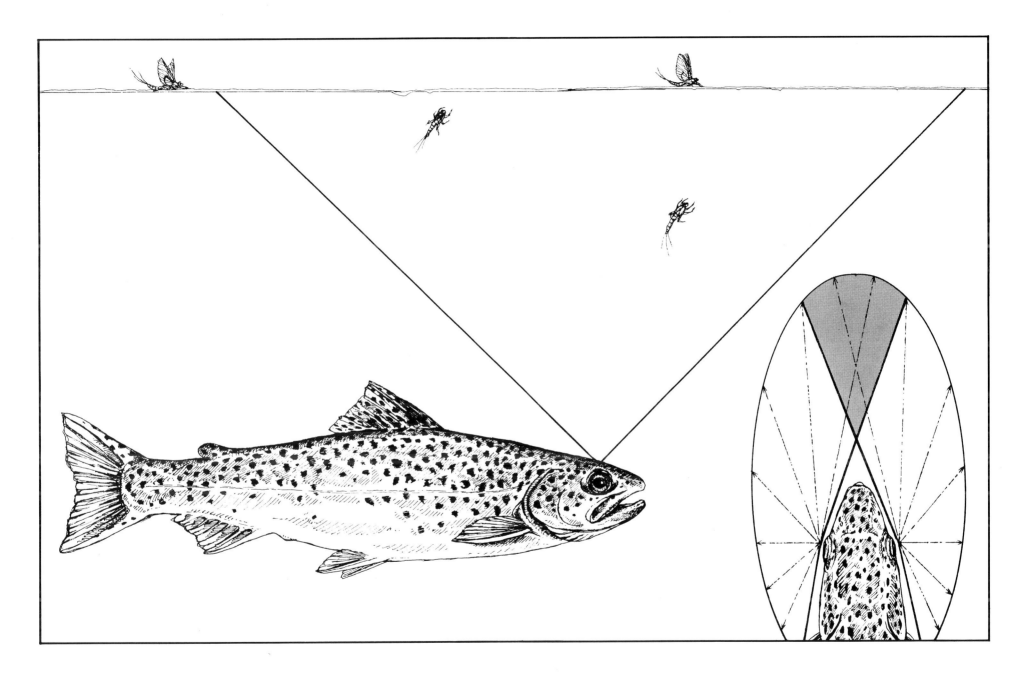

of this opening depends on the fish's depth; at six inches beneath the surface, the window may be no more than six inches across. If he goes deeper, the window will be twice as wide as his depth, but the images will be dimmer since light is absorbed by water.

What can the trout see out of this window? It all depends at what angle light-rays are striking the surface; directly above him, where refraction is zero, he can see objects clearly, but his perception of objects becomes dimmer and more distorted as the angle of the rays from them becomes nearer to the horizon. Peripheral objects seen through the window seem smaller, and an angler at a low angle to the window probably appears squashed, like an image from a fairground's distorting mirror. Distances are also more difficult for the fish to gauge at the edges of his window, so an angler who creeps up in a straight line towards a trout he has spotted will have a much better chance of approaching close without alarming the fish, since his increasing proximity will not be betrayed by a correspondingly obvious increase in size.

The mirrored surround to this skylight means that trout can see any object *under* the surface twice – once in reflection, and once, as it were, *in propria persona*. So, while a wetfly or nymph is visible at a greater distance, it is also a clearer target, whereas (again, always depending on his depth in the water) a trout may not even see a dryfly until it is practically on top of him. What he will notice, though, is anything which penetrates the surface mirror and warns him of an approaching item – the points of a dryfly's hackles do just this; they are designed to imitate the legs of an insect, and must appear as spangled points of light which alert the fish to the possibility that something toothsome and worth investigating is appearing in his window.

The optics of Snell's Window should be tempered by the realization that the surface of water is very rarely calm and, when agitated, the images are broken up into shards, so that the trout is seeing out of the water in a series of flashes, possibly resembling some early cinematographic picture. But it would be wrong to suppose that the trout's system of vision is anything less than extremely efficient. On the whole, the angler should assume that if he can see the fish (unless he is directly below it), then the trout can see him. The fact that it does not at once make for cover is not the point. Also, the different refractive indices of light work both ways, and a trout will be deeper in the water than it appears to be.

In fact, because for millions of years he has depended on it for his survival, the trout's ocular system is specialized and efficient; there are, for instance, certain optic nerves specifically designed to detect eye-like dots on a contrasting background, and this can be of great benefit for the fish when hunting other finny prey. And the angler has traditionally exploited this, with the addition of what one might call 'homing points' in feather and metal lures for most salmonids, such as the much-prized cape-feathers from the Indian junglecock, the waxy 'eye' of which is the staple of many killing trout-lures, along with its aesthetically less pleasing, but equally effective, modern counterparts such as multicoloured eyes painted on leadhead jigs, and the affixing of sections of beading from the chains of bath-plugs.

Winged ant

50

One further point. Brown trout in particular have extremely good night-vision, as do their sea-going cousins. Seatrout can pick out the tiniest of flies against the night sky, as well as being partial to a much larger sunken lure; and fishing at night for resident brownies has become a cult in several waters across the world. It used to be known in Britain as 'bustard fishing', from the traditional method of casting a large Bustard and Yellow wetfly pattern down and across the reaches where recalcitrant brown trout of great size were known to lurk. Stout gut was needed, because such fish mean business on those rare occasions when they decide to feed; and there is a peculiar *frisson* to be enjoyed in the experience of dimly discerning the bow-wave of a large trout leaving its lair to pursue your offering. One thing is certain: the senses of the trout are adapted for its survival to an admirable degree. The trout rarely misses a trick.

Rainbow chasing a sedge (caddis)

TROUT, FOOD AND FLIES

The manner of the fishes taking flies, which is by rising to the surface of the water, and sometimes out of it, gives the Angler a very agreeable surprise.

Richard Bowlker: *THE ART OF ANGLING*

As angling literature has frequently reflected, the world of the fish is a predatory republic similar in many ways to our own, but while it is understandable to think of the tyrannical pike as some kind of freshwater shark, or the voracious perch as a brightly uniformed warrior laying into the ranks of smaller fry, the trout seems somehow to be an altogether more civilized feeder.

In fact, the trout is a largely carnivorous and highly active predator, and his physique and verve are accounted for by his high-protein diet. Although the greater part of his food is aquatic, the trout is a catholic feeder and his taste is not confined to flies. Shrimps, snails, daphnia (water-flea), crawfish, terrestrial items such as caterpillars, beetles, slugs, spiders and even certain berries in season are all on the menu. Tadpoles and frogs are also favoured – Beatrix Potter's Mr Jeremy Fisher escaped being swallowed by the Trout only because it did not like the taste of his mackintosh, though it did gobble up his galoshes – and in flood conditions, when such small deer are washed into the current, they will even go for mice. Indeed, fishing with an articulated mouse-fly is an accepted practice for Alaskan rainbows.

Trout can turn cannibalistic, beginning with their fondness for eggs at spawning time, but their piscatorial diet is usually concentrated on the adults and fry of other species; a list of the fish that trout eat around the world would be a long one, but they include minnows, sculpins, alewife and sticklebacks, and the fry of numerous coarse fish such as bream, perch and rudd. Lake trout can go crazy for these gigantic shoals of fry, especially in the autumn when they often hunt them in a pack, herding them into bays, crashing into their densely packed masses and returning to mop up those stunned or disabled. In salmon rivers, too many trout in the headwaters may considerably reduce the chances of the tiny salmon's survival; in Charles Kingsley's *The Water Babies*, Tom asks the salmon why he takes such exception to the trout and is told they are lazy little relations who can't be bothered to go to sea, and have been punished for their idleness by growing small and spotty 'and actually so degraded in their tastes, that they will eat our children'.

Strange things are sometimes found in the stomachs of trout, and it is always worth examining the contents when cleaning the fish. *The Scotsman* in September 1883 reported that a 14-inch yellow trout purchased from a fishmonger in Perth had 'the whole teat of a cow' in its stomach – but this is as nothing compared to a pike reported in the seventeenth century which had 'an infant child in its stomach'! Twigs, weed, stones and feathers are all ingested for various reasons, and the curiosity of the trout led Richard Walker to devise a bizarre pattern. Noticing that some fish (especially those quite recently stocked, and therefore used to feeding on floating pellets in their stews) would rise to the discarded butt of a cigarette, he tied up an 'imitative' pattern called the Filtip, which consisted of a cigarette filter (I believe it had to be a white one) lacquered over with a hook through the middle. However, you don't see many of them in use nowadays. Trout are also quite partial to a piece of picnic bread impaled on the fly and drifted downwind, as certain reservoir rule-breakers know, and I have heard of at least one beat on the famous Test where a grain of maize fished on a small nymph was deemed the only way to tempt the difficult trout in a hatch-pool.

Most trout-fishermen have had to acquire at least a rudimentary knowledge of entomology, because very often it is by no means clear what a trout is feeding upon. There may be several different flies hatching off the water, or there may appear to be none; the trout may be concentrating his attentions upon one of the subaquatic forms like the nymph or pupa, or he may be dining on a tiny fly like the *caenis* or a smut that is invisible from the angler's vantage-point. Until a more precise indication becomes available, one way to guess at the type of fly is to consider the nature of the rise-form being made. As so often with dogmatic sayings, the old dictum that 'you won't catch a fish unless your fly is on the water' can offer most unhelpful advice; it is sometimes better to stop and think.

On the whole, a trout will exert itself to take a food-item only if it offers a high rate of return in proportion to the energy value when ingested, so that the more vigorous the rise, the larger the item is likely to be. A slashing rise usually indicates a sizeable mouthful such as a skittering sedge; a long, exciting bow-wave is typical of the trout chasing another fish, and so on. But this should by no means be taken as a rule of thumb. Nor is it true that big fish will make the mightiest rises: an energetic splash may well be the sign of an over-enthusiastic but undersized trout, while the quiet sip under the far bank may be the kiss of a giant. Francis Francis, who was one of the sanest and most balanced of all Victorian writers on trout and who always stressed that versatility was the key to success, noted: 'It is strange how quietly a big fish will often take fly after fly, close to a bank, with only just his upper lip put to the surface to suck in the victim.'

Shrimp (Gammarus)

Big fish do not always make the mightiest rises

Those interested in the varieties of a trout's rise-forms can do no better than obtain a copy of Brian Clarke's classic book, *The Pursuit of Stillwater Trout* (1975), which contains some remarkable photographs of the different varieties he categorizes. These include 'humping', a kind of subsurface head-and-tail movement which suggests the trout is going to intercept some rising item such as a nymph or shrimp; 'tailing', in which the trout is inverted vertically as he noses around in the weeds for shrimps and snails (such fish are especially hard to catch); and that most thrilling of all the forms, the true 'head-and-tail', a leisurely tilting movement which shows you the whole length of the fish (which is usually taking spent spinners) until it disappears with an exquisite curl of its tail, as if from pleasure.

In waters rich in food, trout may be spoilt for choice because they have the option of eating the water-born insect at several stages of its development – the larval form of the sedge, for instance (known in Britain as a caddis at this stage of its life only), makes a tasty mouthful as it crawls by the bottom encased in its camouflage of grit and vegetable stems, whereas the midge is generally taken as a pupa, and olives are popular as duns. Larva, pupa, emerging insect and spent insect (after laying its eggs) are all laid on for the fish, and we shall shortly look at the life-cycle of one particular aquatic insect, the mayfly, as a specific and most spectacular example.

It would be quite impossible to catalogue all the different flies upon which trout feed around the world. In Britain, there are four orders of aquatic insect, to which one needs to add the category of seasonal terrestrials (which can be most attractive in their period) such as the hawthorn, crane-fly, ant, grasshopper and various moths. The largest order is *Ephemeroptera*, or the up-winged flies, which include such important species as the Olives and the Iron Blues. *Trichoptera* are the sedge flies (known in America as caddis even in their adult form), of which there are around 200 species in the British Isles. They have a distinctive roof of folded-back wings when not in flight, and range from the Murragh, or Great Sedge, to specimens no more than 5mm long. They have four wings and no tails; and they can prove of especial interest to fish after dusk, when they hatch in great numbers.

The order *Plecoptera* contains the Stoneflies, a hard-winged, shiny fly which is of interest to the northern angler in its season, but does not feature as frequently in his arsenal as it does for the American fisherman. Lastly, there are the *Diptera*, or flat-winged flies, this order including the mosquito, the housefly, gnats and midges. A little more detail is necessary concerning the midge, for some flyfishermen do not realize just what a staple part of the trout's diet it forms – you seldom find it being fished on the chalk-streams, for instance. There are over 400 species of midge in Britain, and it is the non-biting Chironimids that primarily concern the angler. Fish probably take these flies (known to the flyfishing fraternity as 'buzzers') every day of the year, and big rises are commonly seen throughout the summer when the water is not too cold or rough.

The spectacle of a general rise of trout is the stuff of dreams. It is amazing how a general consensus

A rainbow dining on midges

among a fish population seems to operate as to when such a rise should begin and end, and it is quite uncanny how they can be feeding merrily one moment and then shut down completely, although the flies continue to hatch. This is particularly true of the evening rise on chalk-streams, when the river, which one moment was boiling with trout, suddenly goes dead. No doubt some subtle changes in atmospheric pressure, or the difference in air/water temperatures are responsible, but it is very frustrating when it happens.

The buzzer rise offers the stillwater man his best chance of such a general rise, until the sedges come on later in the season. The chironimid pupa emerges from its larval form (the bloodworm) and wriggles up to the surface to hatch, during which ascent, like all nymphs, it may be intercepted by roving trout. However, they become really vulnerable to trout at the surface film which, if it is calm, is too tough for them to penetrate; so they hang there, trapped in their thousands, suspended like commas from the line of the water, waiting for the trout to erase them at their leisure. The typical rise-form to a buzzer is a gentle, porpoise-like head-and-tail, sometimes accompanied by a smacking

sound; but if the surface is rippled and the insects can emerge more easily, the fish may take them with more dynamism in their attempts to prevent escape, in which case the artificial should not be static but given an occasional draw through the surface.

Let us return to the *Ephemeroptera* and consider one of the greatest of its British manifestations, the mayfly interlude. Although many trout-fishermen may not see a mayfly from one season to the next, since it is localized in both time and place, and changes in ecology have rendered it rarer, its appearance is a legend, and no book on trout would be complete without some special mention of it. The American angler has a wider range of mayflies with which to cope, from the huge *Hexagenia* to the tiny *Baetis*, and there is some difference in nomenclature. Over here, the *baetis* is not a mayfly, but a group of ephemeropterans that includes the Dark Olive; also, there are flies called mayflies in the North Country which are in fact Stoneflies. The chapter that follows is the story of many aquatic flies, writ large. The late Oliver Kite once popped one into his mouth, declaring that what was good for the trout was good enough for him, too.

Sedge (caddis)

Grasshopper

THE DREAM OF AN ALCHEMIST
TROUT AND THE MAYFLY CARNIVAL

Monstrous, but tiny . . .
It's something else –
The dream of an alchemist.

Ted Hughes: SAINT'S ISLAND

For one whole year, or maybe two, they have been living secretly down there in the silt or marl of the waterbed, lemon-pale larvae with feathery gills and capacious mandibles. The fish know about them, and the entomologists, but to the world of the upper air they are hidden until this time of the year when, in certain areas of the British Isles, a mass vertical migration takes place. In their billions the mayfly nymphs surface, take wing, and enact their spectacular moments of destiny.

There are three species of mayfly in this country: *Ephemera danica, E. vulgata* and *E. lineata*. The latter is so rare, and the imago (or final metamorphosis) of the other two so similar, that they can in effect be treated as identical by the layman. They are the largest of the order of day-flies known as the *Ephemeroptera* and, as this name suggests, they seldom survive longer than a day in their winged state. 'Away with him, away with

Heading for the weeds

him! He speaks Latin!' shrieks Shakespeare's Jack Cade – and while one does not wish to be blinded by science, it is just as well to appreciate the distinctive life-cycle of these unmistakable insects.

The mayfly is distributed unevenly across our waters, ranging from the famous chalk-streams in the South of England – Test, Kennet and Lambourn – to the huge limestone loughs of Eire, such as Corrib and Mask. The greenish *danica*, which is the more common, prefers alkaline water and seldom thrives in conditions of great exposure or altitude. *Vulgata*, not as widespread as its name implies, is a browner creature when it first takes flight, and tends to favour more sluggish habitats; it is found in certain counties to the east. Hatches of mayfly are cyclical, and in some years they put in a poor appearance; being very susceptible to pollution, their previous eruptions are now a thing of the past in many waters.

59

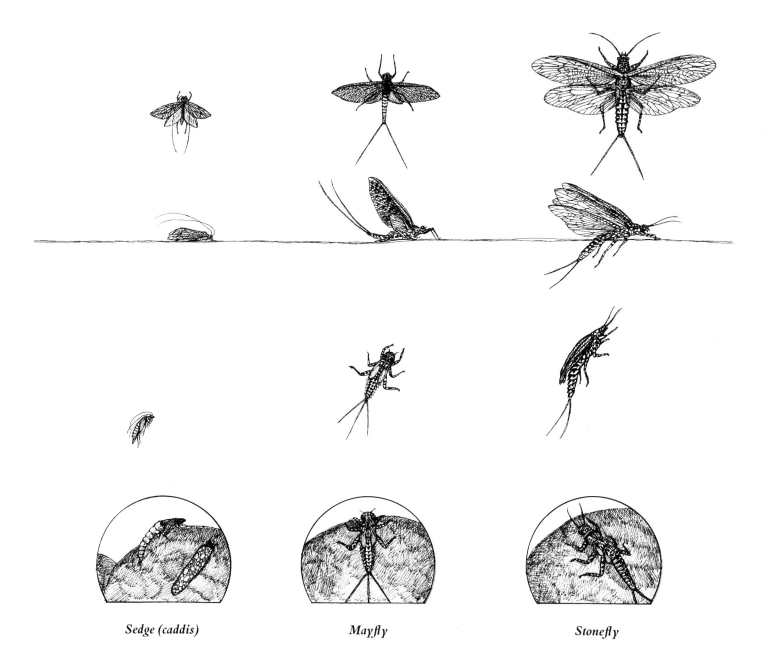

Sedge (caddis)   **Mayfly**   **Stonefly**

According to weather conditions and micro-climate, their seasonal arrival can vary quite considerably, but the main hatches usually coincide with the last few days of May. For the angler, then, a date around 1 June is a fairly safe bet, since by then the trout will have had the chance to become familiar with their massively stocked larders. Hatches normally begin with down-stream reaches of a particular river, and in Ireland the fly first emerges in the south; but if you are going to catch the phenomenon at its peak, you will have to be privy to local knowledge.

So what is it that makes this annual event so remarkable? For the angler, it offers a period (some-times, misleadingly, dubbed the Duffer's Fortnight) when trout can embark on a frenzy of feeding that produces unique opportunities to catch a reluctant specimen. In practice, such red-letter days are far less common than tradition suggests, and the fish can become gorged and choosy with frustrating fre-quency. The chief delight of the Mayfly Carnival is rather the drama enacted by these beautiful flies themselves.

Because the mayfly is so large, the details of its last stages of existence are almost uniquely visible to the naked eye. Though several little sporadic hatches will have occurred previously, the two to three weeks of the hatch proper display much of the wonder and mystique of adaptive evolution, as for a brief spell these insects seem to monopolize the landscape. The nymphs rise to the surface, and there the skin at the back of the thorax splits; with a frantic struggle the legs emerge, and then the two sets of wings, and the creature hauls itself up and out of its filmy prison, pauses to dry, and flies uncertainly to the shelter of the nearest land.

This moment of eclosion is miraculous to observe in any fly; but in this instance it looks like one of those speeded-up films of a plant bursting into flower. The fly that emerges at this stage is called the sub-imago (or 'dun'), but it is not the end of the story, because this genus of fly is unusual in undergoing two different stages of the winged adult. The dun will shortly change once more, and the imago that emerges is the finished and perfect mayfly, a delicate insect with translucent wings, a creamy body measuring some 2cm long, and three long whisks of a tail. At this stage it is known as a 'spinner'.

What ensues is a '*danse d'amour*' that is quite un-forgettable. The males, as in some rural dance-hall, congregate in a position of high visibility, rising and falling in a cloud over the nearby land, until a female sallies forth from the undergrowth and makes herself available. Several may attach themselves to her at any one time, and her eggs are fertilized as they plummet towards the ground, after which act the male soars off back to the dance and the lone female hurries to the water to lay her eggs.

At this stage of her development, the female mayfly is a remarkable example of biological efficiency. Like the male, her mouth-parts have atrophied (which accounts for the short life of the imago) and her alimentary canal is full of air. Around 6,000 eggs are packed into her body cavity, right up to the point behind her head. She has but one purpose now, and traverses the water, curtseying at intervals on to the surface to wash off deposits of eggs extruded from her

61

abdomen. The males spin on aloft, but she soon expires, her wings flat out upon the current, unresisting victim to trout, even as her future generations drift silently downwards to the safety of the silt.

There is something about the mayfly season which is inescapably romantic. Now that the mass migrations of wildfowl and the panoramic movement of big game linger only as folk memories at best, the sudden and lavish performance of even a lifeform so marginal as this diaphanous insect takes on a new significance. In the teeth of almost everything that threatens its survival – acid rain, the abuse of our watertables, the encroachment of conurbations – the brilliant explosion of the mayfly offers the myth and promise of resurrection. It is the annual realization of a dream come true; and that moment when the slim but stately fly bursts once more into the air is a type of affirmation. Ted Hughes describes it as 'the dream of an alchemist', and the day when such alchemy fails will be a short breath before the final destruction of our countryside. And as such, the remarkable dance of the *danica* is a fitting fable for our time.

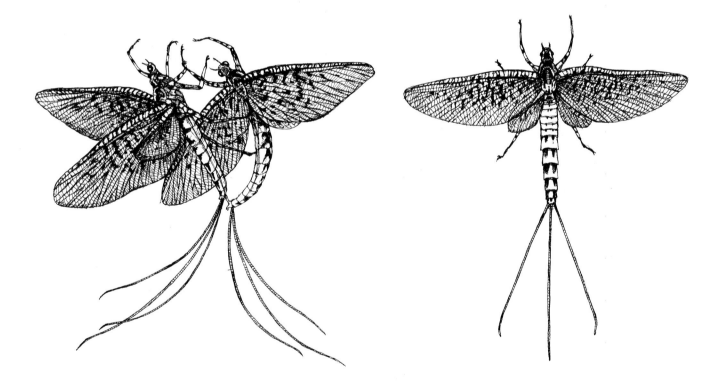

Danse d'amour

Spent spinner

Angling Methods and Developments

I dropped the berry in a stream,
And caught a little silver trout.

W. B. Yeats: *THE SONG OF WANDERING AENGUS*

It is sometimes thought by the unconverted that flyfishing is a method that makes catching trout more difficult, and that this is part of its challenge; but in fact the use of the artificial fly can be every bit as deadly as natural bait, and of course when the fish are preoccupied with a hatch it is *the* killing method. So it is not surprising to learn that, while our earliest angling ancestors must have relied on bait, there is evidence that the artificial fly has been around for at least 1,700 years.

It was a Greek writer of the third century A.D., Claudius Aelianus, who made the first allusion extant to fishing with the fly as practised by the Macedonians in the River Astraeus, but he is tantalizingly unsure about the type of fish: 'Now there are in it fishes of a speckled hue, but what the natives call them, it is better to inquire of the Macedonians', he writes; but his description of how they engulf the fly, 'like a wolf bearing a sheep away from the fold', makes them sound very like trout. There is some possibility that Aelian poached many of his remarks from a writer who had lived two centuries previously, which puts him at the head of a distinguished line of literary plagiarists in the angling world.

It was not until the last century, with the rage for specialization, that angling writers devoted entire books to the trout; until then, works on fishing tended to be comprehensive and offer advice about all freshwater species. The first modern classic was also one of the first books printed in English, *A Treatyse of Fysshynge with an Angle* which was appended to *The Boke of St Albans* (1496). Much print has been made over to the matter of the authorship of this seminal and remarkably durable work, but it has all been inconclusive, and it remains attributed to Dame Juliana Berners, supposedly Prioress or Abbess of Sopwell. It

would be nice to imagine this robust and influential work having come from the pen of such a lady, but it may well be that she did not even exist.

Berners records twelve different fly patterns (or 'dubs') but stresses they are for use only when fish are rising; at other times, the trout should be taken with caterpillars or grubs. She describes the trout as 'a right deyntous fyssh and also a right fervente byter', and offers instruction about how to dye and prepare horsehair for the line – she advocates six hairs, which was heavy tackle indeed, even for her day.

Where flyfishing is concerned, the development of refined techniques was hampered for centuries by the limitations of the tackle. The 'lyne of one or two herys' of Berners' era was still in use in the eighteenth century (John Gay refers to horsehair lines in his *Rural Sports*: 'While all your Hope hangs on a single Hair'), and such lines of twisted and knotted horsehair were difficult to cast. The result was something like a blowline that had to be fished up- or downstream to the trout according to the wind, and was attached directly to the point of a long wooden rod. Reels did not come into use in Europe until after the Restoration of 1660. Another problem was getting a fly to float properly, and though Leonard Mascall as early as 1590 had suggested making their bodies out of cork, the idea did not take hold.

Given these technical shortcomings, that expert trout angler, Charles Cotton, seems none the less to have anticipated several more modern aspects of the sport. Izaak Walton's aristocratic young protégé (the distinction between 'Mr Izaak Walton' and 'Charles Cotton Esquire' is notable on the title-page of the fifth edition of *The Compleat Angler* of 1676, to which Cotton added his observations on trout) fished the clear waters of the Derbyshire Dove by his home at Beresford Hall. He was quite scientific in his approach to the trout, inspecting their gorges to ascertain which fly they were taking, listing some sixty dressings, developing new dubbings on to silk. 'To fish fine and far off is the first and principal rule for trout-angling', he wrote, and he tapered his line from seven down to two hairs accordingly.

Walton himself was by all accounts not much of a flyfisher; he gave Cotton one of his patterns, which he promptly 'hung in his parlour window to laugh at'; but Cotton reckoned him to be the best man in the kingdom at fishing with the natural minnow. Walton also used an artificial one 'that will catch a Trout as well as an *artificial Flie*, and it was made by a handsom Woman that had a fine hand, and a live *Minnow* lying by her'. There was no sign there of any purism: this did not seem to cross any angler's mind until the advent of the Victorian era.

Two quite different areas of trouting interest belong to the last century. The habit of fashionable families to visit Scotland for the summer sport (a vogue that went in tandem with the popularity of tweed, whisky and the works of that accomplished angler, Sir Walter Scott) meant that fishing Highland rivers and lochs began to receive some attention in print. From the middle of the last century date many of our classic wetfly patterns; and we see writers like W. C. Stewart arguing powerfully for the use of spider patterns fished upstream to avoid spooking the trout on the hard-fished Lowland waters where he plied his line.

Brown trout rising to a sherry spinner

65

In the 1870s, however, there began the cult of the dry-fly, something which was to last until the Great War and beyond. There were two main factors responsible for this, the most peculiar and irrational example of idolatry in the history of the sport. First, there were far-reaching improvements in available tackle; rods made of split-cane, more manoeuvrable lines of oiled silk, and the manufacture of eyed hooks (available from 1879, and the invention of H. S. Hall who, along with G. S. Marryat, also produced patterns that would turn over properly in the air) made floating-fly fishing a real prospect. Gut from silkworms for casts had been in use for some time (Pepys has an entry in his diary for 1667: 'This day Mr Caesar told me a pretty experiment of his, of Angling with a Minikin, a gut-string varnished over, which keeps it from swelling and is beyond any hair for strength and smallness – the secret I like mightily'); but the problem of the eyeless hook was that the gut loop had to be whipped along the body, which made it heavy.

The second factor was an interest in classification and taxonomy that was typical of the Victorian mind, and which led to a minute study of the flylife of the chalk-streams of the south. Pioneering work had been done by Alfred Ronalds, whose *The Flyfisher's Entomology* was published in 1836, and included experiments into the taste-buds of trout using natural flies smeared with mustard or honey; but the great standard-bearer of what became known as the 'natural imitation' school was F. M. Halford.

The essence of his belief was that the only sporting way of catching a trout on the southern rivers was by matching as closely as possible the floating fly on which it was feeding. Halford was the historian, rather than the inventor, of this rigorous code of practice, and he certainly contributed a great deal to our knowledge of insects in the seven books he published. The problem is that he became increasingly dogmatic and intransigent, refusing to believe that any method other than the upstream dry-fly could be countenanced by a genuine sportsman – the wet-fly, for example, was dangerous, useless or wrong. His attitudes are best set out in his 1889 volume *Dryfly Fishing in Theory and Practice*, which is at least readable – if appropriately dry – but by the end of his life he had become entrenched and embattled against those who queried his absolute prescriptions, and the very title of his last book, *The Dry-fly Man's Handbook* (1913) suggests that he believed he was addressing a select and superior order of men.

We should not be too hard on Halford and his disciples, nor turn back too strongly the current of opinion, for there is no doubt that the dry-fly is a precise, deadly and intriguing art form – everything that happens is in full view of the angler, and it is perhaps the most theatrical of all methods of fishing for trout with a fly. It is just that the very notion of 'exact imitation' is impracticable, given the problems of reproducing on a metal hook such features as the translucency of an insect's body. The opposing school of thought is, crudely put, the 'presentation' school, which holds that accuracy of casting, speed of movement, and timing are more important than close imitation. And one of the first eloquent exponents of this was G. E. M. Skues.

Halford and Skues crossed swords because the latter

The artificial pattern must compete with the natural fly

insisted that by fishing over rising trout with a close approximation of the *subsurface* insect form they were taking, using his nymphs and adapted spider patterns, he was being just as sporting, and somewhat more practical, than the purists. Skues put forward his case persuasively in two books, *Minor Tactics of the Chalk Stream* (1910) and *The Way of a Trout with a Fly* (1921); and if they are both more readable than anything penned by his opponent, it is because as a writer he is a less infallible and didactic companion – a consideration of paramount importance in assessing the value of a fishing volume.

While this skirmishing was under way in the lush water-meadows of the elite, most anglers were continuing to fish for trout according to the conditions of their local water. On the whole it is still true that the wet-fly, whether up- or downstream, is better suited to rougher streams such as those of the North or the West Country, where you search out the likely lies without waiting for some hatch to match. On some waters you would wait for months before such a phenomenon occurred. On the richer streams, though, it is quite proper and feasible to cast to individually rising fish from a downstream vantage-point, to escape detection; and this selective method will avoid spooking other trout in the clear water. In deciding his tactics (where rules will permit either, of course) the angler should be guided by practicality.

It was not the ethics but the practicality of the dry-fly that effected its introduction to North America, where its use was pioneered by Theodore Gordon, founder of the Catskill School of Flydressers. Since there was already a gradual decline in the eastern rivers that anglers had traditionally fished for native brookies, logging and drainage having raised the temperature and altered the watertables, improved transport and increased angling pressure were beginning to have a serious effect on the numbers of trout available. The days of the happy-go-lucky streamer fisherman were numbered, as trout (especially the cannier brownie) became more wary and difficult to tempt. The delicate finesse of the dry-fly technique was therefore adopted as a more killing tactic, and was further popularized by George La Branche who developed several patterns of duns and caddis and who explained how to 'fish the water' in his lovely little book *The Dry Fly and Fast Water* (1914).

It goes without saying that angling techniques are constantly in a state of flux, and nowadays a year seldom goes by without some expert producing an entire book dedicated to one specific aspect of fly-fishing for trout. There are also so many artificial patterns that dictionaries of dressings can scarcely keep up to date, and one has to take care not to become baffled by the whole business. Although it is tempting to be equipped with the latest 'wonder fly', many anglers stick with entire confidence to quite a small repertoire of patterns, concentrating on presentation and watercraft and persistence rather than gimmickry. It would be wrong to suggest that any single method of flyfishing for trout is today more skilful than another, for the really accomplished angler is an all-rounder. First-class dry-fly fishing for trout is a rare commodity in our more populous regions, and few anglers will pass by the chance of a day on such a water. Contrary to legend, you do not have to wear

A hatch on the chalk stream

a leather kneeling-pad and pronounce the name of your fish 'trite' to be a dry-fly angler. Nor does being a nymph-fisherman automatically brand you a bounder. The upstream nymph is without doubt one of the subtlest forms of flyfishing, demanding great concentration, keen eyesight, immaculate timing and a certain sixth sense into the bargain, if a decent proportion of trout are to be hooked. You have to gauge the depth and flow of the stream, be prepared to cast weighted flies on long leaders, and respond to the slightest arresting of the line's progress or dimly perceived flash of a trout's flank under the water. It would take a Halford not to be spellbound by its challenge.

Mention should here be made of the stillwater revolution which has occurred during the last two decades in Britain. Public angling has been allowed in certain reservoirs for many years now: Lake Vyrnwy in Wales opened in 1891, Ravensthorpe in North-amptonshire in 1893, and the beautiful Blagdon in Somerset in 1904. Although some developments were made by Dr Bell of Blagdon fame in designing patterns specifically to imitate the flies on which stillwater trout fed, it was initially the use of salmon-flies as lures, and traditional Scottish wet-flies such as the Alexandra and Peter Ross, which prevailed.

In 1966, Grafham Water reservoir in Huntingdon opened with a bonanza that gave the refinement of stillwater techniques a welcome boost; the develop-ment of specialist tactics from deep-sunk lures, through broadside drifting, to the imitation of tiny nymphs, has since become a distinct branch of the sport, along with the many flyfishing competitions held at such waters each year. Stillwater flyfishing is now big business, and there are also dozens of newly created smaller waters that have become well-established venues for hunting specimen trout.

We have already mentioned Avington, but there are also the nearby Damerham, which has a justified reputation for big rainbows taken from its small, almost aquarial lakes, Rockbourne Trout Fishery, Newbury Lake in Berkshire, Chalk Springs by Arundel, and many more. Fishing for the trout in these lakes is an experience quite different from that of a reservoir or loch, where you will be fishing a team of flies over the front of a boat, or casting far from the bank. In these little lakes, however artificial they may be, the fish are nearly all within casting range, and the clear water soon makes them nervous. They will come to a dry-fly at times (the truth is that many anglers don't even try the method), but generally they are best tempted on a weighted nymph drawn carefully up into their path as they cruise. Given that you may well see rainbow trout into double figures during the day, it is as well to have nerves of steel. Such fishing is by no means to everyone's taste: there are many who prefer to fish in the wild for genuinely wild trout, or not to fish at all. I, too, have my preferences, but the foremost of these is to fish for trout of whatever type, in whatever water, rather than twiddle my thumbs in the metropolis. Those who sneer at the stocked trout as being tame and easy to catch are often speaking from ignorance; you can learn a lot about the be-haviour of fish by visiting such places, and that is always likely to prove an advantage in the end.

Baitfishing for trout has a long pedigree, but it has *A fatal attraction*

to be said that it cannot be rated very highly as a sporting method if practised indiscriminately. There is little skill involved in dragging a fish from pond or brook on floatfished worms, unless the water level is unusually low, in which case it is a fine business, and one for the expert with his long rod, light tackle, and sure touch as he casts his hook upstream and feels it venture down, searching out the contours of the river bed. At the slightest knock he will tighten, and it is astonishing how often the hook will come flying back naked towards him. Quite how the trout is able to suck a carefully threaded worm off a bait rig is a mystery, but the angler who makes a good bag with such tackle is a master in his own right.

Spinning for trout is popular in North America, and in France and Scandinavia, but I have had little cause to try it in Britain. It is a relatively recent method, since the first reliable reel made for the purpose was not developed until the 1880s by the Scot, Peter Malloch. Then, towards the end of the century, Alfred Illingworth, a woollen manufacturer, came up with a design for the fixed-spool reel, an open-faced model that has been refined today into a weapon of great versatility. The closed-face reel, or spincast model, in which the spool housing the nylon is covered by a hood, is an American invention that has made spinning for trout a method the rudiments of which most bunglers can grasp in a matter of minutes.

Some trout, particularly those living deep in still waters, such as lakers or ferox, can be reached by anglers much of the time only if they troll for them. This involves dragging a lure behind a boat until something hooks itself; nowadays the angler often keeps his eyes fixed on the screen of a sonar device which will tell him the depth and speed of his lure and may display fish on a coloured screen. This seems to me to be about as far from the spirit of angling as one can go. I would prefer to read a good book.

If we ignore the purely technical books on the subject, I think it can be claimed that good piscatorial writing has something in common with imaginative literature, the reader not just being lectured to, but drawn into and involved in the world evoked by the book. A classic fishing book is therefore more than the sum of its parts; and it is also about more than fishing alone. To be durable rather than just a piece of period interest, at its heart it must be concerned with things that do not change, such as the relationship between man and fish, man and the environment. The novelist John Buchan wrote this about angling verse, 'For it has to do, not with passing fashions and outworn creeds, but with the great things of the world . . .'

This sounds a bit of a tall order, but such a quality over and above the specifics concerning the business of casting for fish is readily noticeable when you encounter it. It accounts for the enduring status of, for instance, *The Compleat Angler*, of which there have been some 400 editions, although for some reason it has lately become fashionable to denigrate it. For the most part, one would not read it today for advice about technique, but this splendid example of English pastoral prose is not only an evocation of an idyllic order of vanished Albion, it also exudes a sense of personality. And this is a necessary quality for a good book on the subject.

Not every reader admires what can be described as

Spring rainbow chasing three-spined sticklebacks

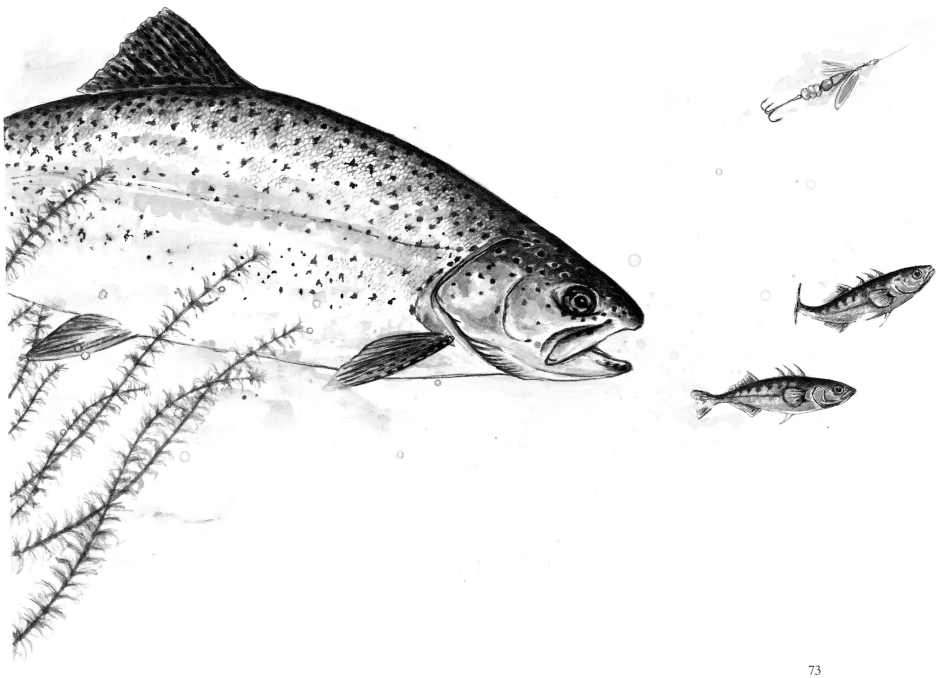

the cumbersome and erudite prose style of Walton, and Cotton's sometimes tongue-in-cheek imitation of it. But the great quality of the book is that it is reflective and digressive at the same time, and is suffused with a love for its subject. It is the archetype of the fishing classic because it re-creates, through its audio-visual effects, the very experience of being at the waterside. This is not as easy to do as some writers have imagined. It is not enough to be merely anecdotal, though angling is a pastime which has a natural affinity with the telling of stories; the writer must have an eye for significant detail, the sort of observation that encapsulates the essence of the sport.

Despite the fact that its own literature is traditionally supposed to be well stocked with inventions, it is curious how little really good fiction has been written about fishing. Both Hemingway and Norman Maclean have written outstanding stories about trout-fishing, Richard Brautigan wrote a hipster novel surrounding the image, and David James Duncan produced a cult book that went way over the top in its efforts to be all things to all anglers; but on the whole the best evocative descriptions belong in fishing books proper.

Here is T. H. White explaining how the sound of a cuckoo always translates him back to a day on the River Coln: 'Cuckoo, it said, twice: and there on my fingers was the sticky, the grassy, the fishy smell of trout. There were his rosy stipples, his buck in the hand, the olive dun in the tender nook of his lip. The gut gets in the way as you make to disgorge. He was in my nose and ear and spine.' And what could be more vivid a lament for the extinct trout of the Yarrow than this tribute from Stoddart? It was, he remembers, 'a lovely fish, ornate with a rare sprinkling of stars, darker than crimson, and these on a light amber ground, which shaded off towards the belly, became gradually like mother-of-pearl. The head was small, the back curved, and the fins yellow, as a newly minted guinea.'

In terms of antiquity and sheer volume, fishing literature beats all other sports hands down. In the Fearing Library Collection at Harvard, there are said to be more than 12,000 books on the subject. Inferior piscatorial literature is not uncommon, of course, and the things that make it bad are the same elements that flaw any literary work: jargon, pedantry, sloppiness, lack of humour, a throbbing vein of dogma, mawkishness, and fanatical enthusiasm which causes obscurity and an over-run of language. But at its best it is quite simply a tribute to man's love for fish.

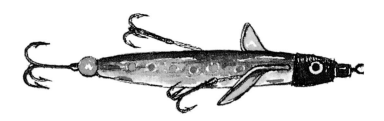

THE NEXT THING TO DREAMING
THE MENTALITY OF THE TROUT-FISHER

And angling does indeed seem the
next thing to dreaming.

James Henry Leigh Hunt: *THE INDICATOR AND THE COMPANION*

It is often said that there is more to fishing than just catching fish ('*Piscator non solum piscatur*'), but one might be forgiven for wondering just what these other factors are. How can one profess to have had a good day, if you return empty-handed?

It should be said from the start that all anglers prefer to catch fish when they go out, and the fake sportsman who professes indifference ('I don't care if I catch one or not – it's just nice to be out on the water') is an arrant liar. But actually landing a fish is not the *sine qua non* of the process. My most memorable day's trout-fishing was not the one on which I caught the most, or even the time I caught my largest trout; it was, in fact, a day on which I caught nothing. It was sultry and close, and I was fishing the two lakes at Latimer Park in Buckinghamshire where I used to have a regular rod when I was a student. These lakes are generally clear and well stocked with browns and rainbows up to a

large size, which you can see patrolling in between patches of weed. I was having no success with the usual small nymphs, the fish ignoring my best efforts, so I decided to try a pattern I had concocted the night before – an outlandish confection of latex rubber and seal's fur.

I am never sure which is the more boring, fishing stories in which everything goes according to plan, or those when one got away – but in this case I qualify on both counts. In the space of two hours I had takes from seven large rainbows that clearly had never seen anything like my nymph before and whose jaded palates were sharpened by its curious appearance. In every case, something went wrong; either I struck too soon or too late, or the hook-point broke, or the fish took to the air and threw the fly. I returned to the lodge full of regrets, but conscious of the intense excitement I had experienced for two hours. I had

been transported by that peculiar combination of relaxation and concentration that every angler knows, and at least I had had the satisfaction of fooling seven fish with an invention of my own, when few others were having any action at all. The fact that the rainbows had the last laugh was my fault, and I put it down to experience over a tumbler or two of malt. But I believe I can remember each of those takes distinctly today, and the complex emotions aroused by the anticipation and frustration are almost as keen now as they were a decade ago.

There is also an aesthetic pleasure to be had from the mere process of casting in itself. The rhythm and timing required to make consistently long and accurate casts, allowing for the wind and the drag of the current, are as difficult to master as a golf-swing; and if, at the end of the day, you return fishless, then at least you will have had the satisfaction of knowing that you were fishing well. Indeed, just handling the tackle is a source of pleasure to most trout anglers, for rods, reels and flies seem to have an intrinsic appeal which is more than just functional beauty. A well-turned, precision-made reel by Hardy or Marryat, a tiny one-weight Orvis carbon rod or some antique wand of Palakona cane are exquisite objects, however battle-scarred. A venerable flybox of black japanned tin, a wicker creel, or a mahogany 'priest' are a joy for the angler just to have about his person.

Angling enjoyment is a series of personal rituals that begin before you arrive at the bankside. Before you set forth, there is the delicious anticipation of sorting through your gallimaufry of tackle, considering each item, imagining the next day's sport, wondering if

The rainbows had the last laugh – throwing the fly

you will regret not taking that extra spool with the sinking line, that short rod for roll-casting under the trees. Arming for the fray quickens the angler's blood as, like some jouster or gladiator, he assembles his mysterious weaponry, full of superstition about his precious talismans such as his battered hat and his waistcoat strung with spring-loaded devices. By the time he kneels to try the first trout, the fisherman has already enjoyed himself very much indeed.

Subsidiary pleasures do include an appreciation of the surroundings, of course, especially when the angler can relax with a trout or two in his creel. Anglers are fond of the good life, and many writers take care to remind their readers of the need to look after the inner man. Patrick Chalmers, in his charming book *At the Tail of the Weir* (1932), gives advice as to the best type of post-prandial cigar, and one relishes the self-portrait of Hemingway on the Rhône with his catch of trout, happily eating 'a paperbagful of cherries'. As early as 1676, William Gilbert advised that essential equipment included 'a good Neats-Tongue, and a Bottle of Canary', while the opera singer Harry Plunket Greene's memory of Blagdon is as much to do with his meal of wild duck and cider as it is with the lake's huge trout.

But the heart of the matter is that the angler is for the most part absorbed in his thoughts about trout, and what he cannot see he must imagine. Much of an angler's fishing takes place inside his head, and he is immersed in a continuous dream of a world under water. So intensely does he concentrate on the business that he tries to project his mind into his quarry's element, until the mentality of hunter and hunted

77

become almost interchangeable. In short, the trout-fisherman spends his day being the nearest thing he can become to a trout itself. Like the sage, Chuang-Tzǔ, who dreamed he was a butterfly and could not be sure, when he awoke, whether or not he was a butterfly dreaming of being a man, this private, watery dream-scape of the trout angler becomes an integral part of his perception of the world.

This dream is not just the mundane fantasy of catching a fish, but the expression of something older, deeper and more complex. Nor is it just the revival of some ancient instinct for hunting. Time and again in literature you come across the notion that the sub-surface world is both a reflection and an inversion of our own, not only an element into which we peer with fascination, but also an element from which we are observed, and in which we see ourselves. 'Fish die belly-upward and rise to the surface,' wrote André Gide in his *Journals*, 'it is their way of falling.' Melville compared it to the legend of Narcissus, 'that same image, we ourselves see in all rivers and oceans. It is the image of the ungraspable phantom of life . . .'

When trout-fishers meet on the bank, they generally inquire if the other has had any luck, action or success; what they do not ask is whether you are enjoying yourself, for the question would be an entirely super-fluous one. Anglers can enjoy fishing for trout when they are stuck in traffic jams or trenches or desert outposts. And that is the whole point of a dream-world; a cool, calm dimension where the mind of the angler floats among the images of the fish he has conjured from the shadows.

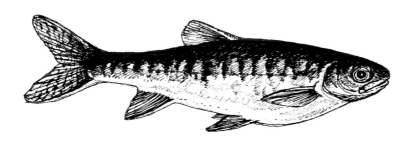

The world according to trout

Minnow

The Ethics of Angling

A filthy, base, illiberal employment, having neither wit
nor perspicacity in it, nor worth the labour.

Plutarch (on fishing): MORALIA

There was a time when anglers were generally held to be persons of probity. One Victorian, hauled before the magistrate for being abroad on the streets at a suspiciously early hour of the day, excused himself simply by saying, 'Sir, I am a roach-fisher.'

As we have seen, anglers are left to their own devices about how they wish to try for their trout, within legal limits for that water, and this freedom of choice is important. But fishing is not a game, in the sense that its rules are discovered rather than devised; and, as the philosopher J. W. Dunne explained, 'your opponent is no less a personage than *Nature herself*', which is really the central challenge.

But there has crept into angling circles in the last few decades an altogether unsavoury attitude of competitiveness, not so much with the fish as with other anglers. As part of the 'biggest is best' attitude of the New Materialism, there is growing discontent among many trout-fishermen with fish of less than, say, two pounds, on most stocked waters, and a feeling that, if you don't catch your limit bag, then somehow you have failed. While the idea of quotas is generally sound, the habit of calibrating success by numbers (encouraged in the angling media by pictures of 'famous' trout anglers displaying huge numbers of dead fish) is a pernicious one that equates the death of the trout with the purpose of the expedition. And this has got out of hand.

It used to be said that an angler went through three phases in his career: trying first to catch the most trout, then the largest trout, and then the most difficult trout. It would be a shame if the latter category fell into disregard amid concern about value for money and the average weight of fish caught by rods each week.

For some time now there has existed on certain American streams an enlightened policy of 'catch-

and-release' that operates no-kill stretches and ensures a massive stock of trout, many of which, having once been caught, are more difficult to tempt. Those who are suspicious of the advantages of this system claim that fish are likely to be returned in a damaged or exhausted state, and will die or contract fungal diseases; but surveys have shown an extremely low mortality rate, and there are suggestions that trout can be caught several times in a season.

Some anglers simply cannot see the point in landing a fish unless it is going to be killed, and they cite the old 'hunter-gatherer' argument about man's natural instinct for predation. Personally, I am more than happy to return trout to the water, retaining the occasional one to give to friends; but in England a lot of public-access waters have a rule specifying that all fish landed must be killed.

The reason for this is that British anglers have been slow to learn about the correct methods of handling a fish that is to be released, though the fact is coarse fishermen have been practising this for a very long time, and individual pike and carp of recognizable appearance are caught regularly several times every season, having put on weight in the meantime. There is also a myth that you have to fish with barbless hooks and this means you will lose more trout. Provided you keep a tight line once your fish is on (and a prayer to St Zeno, the patron saint of fish-hooks, seldom goes amiss here), a barbless hook is no more likely to come adrift than any other; and if it means you are going to play the fish more gently (thus prolonging its stress) then you are better off with a conventional barbed one.

A fish that is to be released should be brought in as soon as is reasonably possible. This sounds like a truism, but many anglers claim to gauge their enjoyment of fishing by the duration and acrobatics of the fight, which I find incomprehensible. Of course it is disappointing if a trout comes in sluggishly once hooked, like some chub, but in this case it will be because it is badly out of condition. As far as I am concerned, my primary aim is to get a fish into the net, and, to effect this, I will use the strongest nylon practical without risking the spooking of the fish in the first place, and the greatest pressure I can bring to bear without courting the disaster of a break or the hook tearing out, both of which are angling crimes, where avoidable. The sooner the trout is to hand, the better his chances of safe recovery. Ideally, you should slide him into a landing net made of knotless mesh, hold him firmly but without squeezing, and slide your free hand down the leader to disengage the fly. The fish should not be removed from the water or gripped with dry hands.

If the fish is tired, hold it with its head into the current until it revives, or move it gently, head first, in a circle through still water until it is able to swim steadily away. A fish that shoots away may well turn belly-up shortly after, and one that is bleeding from the gills will not survive and must be killed.

Many anglers are too light on their fish and do not realize the potential of their own tackle. The American angler, Lee Wulff, has for decades been demonstrating this point by using lighter and lighter tackle to beat large fish, but this should not be attempted by those who lack the confidence to land the fish in a reasonable time. Wulff has even caught a ten-pound Atlantic

salmon using just his hands and a fly-reel, and he is no ordinary angler. But all of us have a responsibility towards our fish, once hooked, to land it with the minimum of trauma, whether it is to be kept or not.

For fish do suffer from being caught, largely because they are exhausted and scared at being pulled off balance. They have a sense of touch, too, but I doubt if they feel much of what we would call pain. You can satisfy yourself about the emotive analogies so beloved of anti-fishermen by a simple experiment; next time you are fishing for a trout you can see, let the line go slack as soon as you have hooked him, and keep yourself concealed. The chances are that he will return to his lie without registering the hook in his mouth; but as soon as you exert any *pressure*, he will swim vigorously away from it; and as soon as you reveal your presence, he will become agitated and run. If a trout felt pain, he would follow your pull like a bull with a rope through his nose-ring; but in practice he fights it doggedly. I for one have caught a trout on the Test that had two of my own nymphs in the side of his mouth, like campaign medals, from earlier in the day. Of course I am not proud of having broken off on those prior occasions, but the fish had continued to feed with apparent oblivion, and had fallen for the same trick three times.

Angling may be distinguished from other field sports in that the angler retains the option of sparing his quarry. This is something that children should be taught, along with a respect for the wonderful living creature that is momentarily theirs. Above all, they should be educated about the life of the trout before deciding whether to kill it. There can be few sights more satisfying than that of a large trout gliding back through its element. We owe that, at least, to this remarkable and beautiful fish.

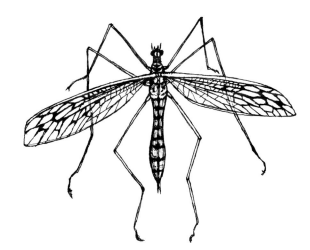

There is more to fishing than killing fish – a true angler has respect for his quarry

Cranefly

83

THREE RECIPES FOR TROUT

There are dozens of fancy recipes for cooking trout, most of which are so elaborate that they disguise the natural flavour of the fish. If it is a wild trout in good condition, it should be cooked as simply and quickly as possible. Nowhere is a trout more delicious than at the waterside itself; here are two basic methods. Clean your fish and wrap it in brown paper or damp newspaper and lay it in the warm ashes of your lunchtime fire, where it will bake in about 30 minutes, and can then be eaten with the fingers. Alternatively, if you have a frying-pan, you can roll the damp fish in a little oatmeal and fry it quickly in some fat or butter, a couple of rashers of bacon making a welcome addition if you have come confident and well prepared.

Trout also make excellent fish-cakes, and this is a good way to use up any leftovers from a larger fish, when cold. Mix together with a fork an equal quantity of baked trout and cold mashed potato, with the addition of some finely chopped parsley, salt and pepper and a little paprika, plus a squeeze of lemon juice. Pat into cakes in the palms of your hands, coat with beaten egg-yolk and cover in breadcrumbs before frying. Again, bacon provides an ideal breakfast accompaniment – although personally I never eat fish before going fishing, out of sheer superstition.

Lastly, for the ambitious, here is a more elaborate and traditional recipe from the 1659 edition of *Barker's Delight*. The author was himself a cook of some distinction, which accounts for his closing criticisms:

The best dish of stewed fish that ever I heard commended of the English, was dressed this way: First they were broiled on a charcole fire, being cut on the side as fried Trouts, then the stew pan was taken and set on a chaffingdish of coles, there was put into the stew-pan half a pound of sweet butter, one penniworth of beaten cinnamon, a little vinegar; when all was melted the fish was put into the pan, and covered with a covering plate, so kept stewing half an hour, being turned, then taken out of the stew-pan and dished, be sure to beat your sauce before you put it on your fish, then squeeze a lemmon on your fish: it was the best dish of fish that ever I heard commended by Noblemen and Gentlemen. This is our English fashion.

There are divers wayes of stewing; this which I set down last was the English way: But note this, that your stewed trouts must be cut on the side: you may make a dish of stewed trouts out of your boyling kettle, stewing of them with the same materialls as I did the broiled trouts, I dare warrant them good meat, and to be very well liked.

The Italian he stews upon a chaffingdish of coles, with whitewine, cloves and mace, nutmegs sliced, a little ginger; you must understand when this fish is stewed, the same liquor that the fish is stewed in must be beaten with some sweet butter and juice of a lemmon, before it is dished for the service. The French doth adde to this a slice or two of bacon, Though I have been no traveller I may speak it, for I have been admitted into the most Ambassadors Kitchins that have come into England this forty years, and do wait on them still at the Lord Protector's charge, and I am paid duly for it: sometimes I see slovenly scullions abuse good fish most grosly.

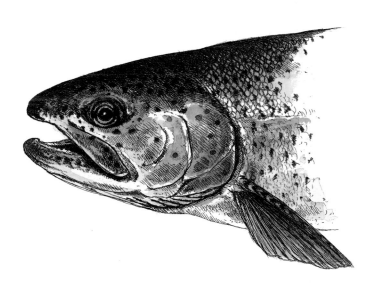

The beſt diſh of ſtewed fiſh that ever I heard commended of the Engliſh, was dreſſed this way: Firſt they were broiled on a charcole fire, being cut on the ſide as fried Trouts, then the ſtew pan was taken and ſet on a chaffingdiſh of coles, there was put into the ſtew-pan half a pound of ſweet butter, one penniworth of beaten cinnamon, a little vinegar; when all was melted the fiſh was put into the pan, and covered with a covering plate, ſo kept ſtewing half an hour, being turned, then taken out of the ſtew-pan and diſhed, be ſure to beat your ſauce before you put it on your fiſh, then ſqueeze a lemmon on your fiſh: it was the beſt diſh of fiſh that ever I heard commended by Noblemen and Gentlemen. This is our Engliſh faſhion.

There are divers wayes of ſtewing, this which I ſet down laſt was the Engliſh way: But note this, that your ſtewed trouts muſt be cut on the ſide: you may make a diſh of ſtewed trouts out of your boyling kettle, ſtewing of them with the ſame materialls as I did the broiled trouts, I dare warrant them good meat, and to be very well liked.

The Italian he ſtews upon a chaffingdiſh of coles, with whitewine, cloves and mace, nutmegs ſliced, a little ginger; you muſt underſtand when this fiſh is ſtewed, the ſame liquor that the fiſh is ſtewed in muſt be beaten with ſome ſweet butter and juice of a lemmon, before it is diſhed for the ſervice. The French doth adde to this a ſlice or two of bacon. Though I have been no rraveller I may ſpeak it, for I have been admitted into the moſt Ambaſſadors Kitchins that have come into England this forty years, and do wait on them ſtill at the Lord Protector's charge, and I am paid duly for it: ſometimes I ſee ſlovenly ſcullions abuſe good fiſh moſt groſly.

Wherein are discovered many rare secrets very necessary to be known by all that delight in that recreation, both for catching the fish, and dressing thereof

AFTERWORD
BY ALAN JAMES ROBINSON

This book is a tribute to that frigid morning thirty years ago when, in Connecticut on 'opening day', I learned at the hands of my father about the joy of trout. First through angling and then, later, through flyfishing, I grew to understand the bonds between father and son, friend and friend, and man and nature. From that time onward, my enthusiasm never diminished – not when I went fishing for those freshly stocked Brooks, Browns and Rainbows in the rambling Mill River of my childhood; not when pursuing the wild trout of the no-name creeks around New England and certainly not with those awesome fish of the famed rivers of the West.

Since the age of five, I've pursued the jewel-sided Brookie in the mountain streams of New Hampshire and Vermont and the brooks of Massachusetts, where nature hides them under bushy snags in the most inaccessible places, reluctantly giving them up. In Montana, I've spent hours casting over the Rainbows of Armstrong Creek, the fish daring me to dupe them with the 'perfect' fly and 'perfect' cast by finning their way blatantly along the canyons of moss beds at my feet. I have derived endless pleasure – and frustration – from hunting the sulking Browns of the undercut banks of the Bighorn River and the 'cruisers' of the subterranean eelgrass forests of the Railroad Ranch area of the Snake River. Most recently, in England, I have had the privilege of walking the banks of a beat on the fabled Test, casting sedges to the bank-feeding Rainbows, and offering fresh-water shrimp patterns to the bottom-skulking Browns.

My search usually extends the whole day, from the mists of morning through the afternoon's heat to the chill of evening. A season for some of the luckier fishermen may last an entire year, but for me it lasts at least from nymphing the icy waters of April, to matching the hatch on a warm June afternoon, to catching a spinner-fall on an August evening, to finally tossing streamers in the autumnal serenity of October.

Through the years I have tried to gain a better understanding of trout by snorkelling rivers and ponds, sometimes earning a clear and unique view of their magical environment. My invasion of the mysterious watery world of trout has made me a keen observer; a good fisherman must be one who employs every sense to discern and discover, to be able to locate and anticipate his quarry. Flyfishing has honed my awareness of nature's complexities as it has quickened my sense of her majesty and her splendour.

Since the early days when my father stood beside me, I have wanted to pay homage to the trout. In this book I have tried to create images that are meant to capture the Brookie's naivete, the Rainbow's vigour, and the Brown's apparent intelligence and all that I have come to know about *TROUT*.

Easthampton
Massachusetts

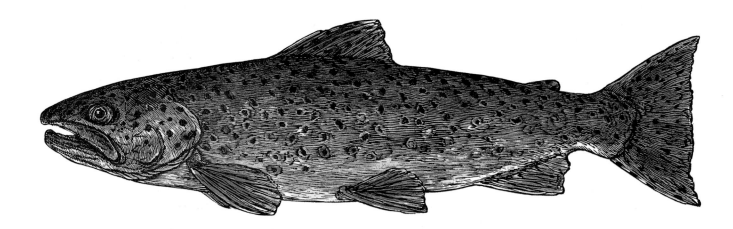

SELECT BIBLIOGRAPHY

Anyone wishing to pursue in greater depth the aspects of trout, and methods of catching them, that have only been touched on in this essay will discover in the following titles a number of useful starting points. Unless specified otherwise, the dates are those of the British editions of each work.

Ray Bergman: *Trout* (1950)
Dame Juliana Berners (attrib.): *A Treatyse of Fysshynge with an Angle* (1496)
Joe Brooks: *Trout Fishing* (1972) New York
Patrick Chalmers: *The Angler's England* (1938)
Charles Chenevix Trench: *A History of Angling* (1974)
Brian Clarke: *The Pursuit of Stillwater Trout* (1975)
J. W. Dunne: *Sunshine and the Dry Fly* (1924)
Hugh Falkus: *Sea Trout Fishing* (1975)
Francis Francis: *A Book on Angling* (1863)

W. E. Frost and M. E. Brown: *The Trout* (1967)
John Gierach: *Trout Bum* (1986) New York
Arnold Gingrich (ed.): *American Trout Fishing* (1966) New York
The Fishing in Print (1974) New York
John Goddard: *Trout Flies of Stillwater* (1979)
John Goddard and Brian Clarke: *The Trout and the Fly* (1980)
F. M. Halford: *Dryfly Fishing in Theory and Practice* (1889)
Cecil E. Heacox: *The Compleat Brown Trout* (1974) New York
J. W. Hills: *A History of Fly Fishing for Trout* (1921) *A Summer on the Test* (1924)
Charles Kingsley: *Chalk Stream Studies* (1859)
G. M. L. La Branche: *The Dry Fly and Fast Water* (1914) New York
Peter Lapsley: *River Trout Fishing* (1988)

A. A. Luce: *Fishing and Thinking* (1959)

Norman Maclean: *Trout and Grayling. An Angler's Natural History* (1980)

Tony Pawson: *Flyfishing Around the World* (1987)

David Profumo and Graham Swift (eds.): *The Magic Wheel* (1985)

Jack Ritchie: *The Australian Trout* (1988) Melbourne

Alfred Ronalds: *The Flyfisher's Entomology* (1836)

Ernest Schwiebert: *Matching the Hatch* (1955)
Trout (1979)

G. E. M. Skues: *Minor Tactics of the Chalk Stream* (1910)
The Way of a Trout with a Fly (1921)

John Solbe: *Water Quality for Salmon and Trout* (1988)

W. C. Stewart: *The Practical Angler* (1857)

Eric Taverner: *Trout Fishing from All Angles* (1929)
Angler's Fishes and Their Natural History (1957)

John Taverner: *Certaine Experiments Concerning Fish and Fruite* (1600)

Conrad Voss Bark: *A Fly on the Water* (1986)

Izaak Walton and Charles Cotton: *The Compleat Angler* (1676)

T. Westwood and T. Satchell: *Bibliotheca Piscatoria* (1883)

Dermot Wilson: *Fishing the Dry Fly* (1987)

Lee Wulff: *Trout on a Fly* (1986) New York